DISCOVERING U.S. HISTORY

Early National America

1790–1850

DISCOVERING U.S. HISTORY

The New World: Prehistory–1542

Colonial America: 1543–1763

Revolutionary America: 1764–1789

Early National America: 1790–1850

The Civil War Era: 1851–1865

The New South and the Old West: 1866–1890

The Gilded Age and Progressivism: 1891–1913

World War I and the Roaring Twenties: 1914–1928

The Great Depression: 1929–1938

World War II: 1939–1945

The Cold War and Postwar America: 1946–1963

Modern America: 1964–Present

DISCOVERING U.S. HISTORY

Early National America
1790–1850

Tim McNeese

Consulting Editor: Richard Jensen, Ph.D.

CHELSEA HOUSE
PUBLISHERS
An imprint of Infobase Publishing

EARLY NATIONAL AMERICA 1790–1850

Chelsea House
An imprint of Infobase Publishing
132 West 31st Street
New York NY 10001

Library of Congress Cataloging-in-Publication Data
McNeese, Tim.
  Early National America, 1790–1850 / written by Tim McNeese.
    p. cm. — (Discovering U.S. history ; v. 4)
  Includes bibliographical references and index.
  ISBN 978-1-60413-351-6 (hardcover)
  1. United States—History—1783–1865—Juvenile literature. I. Title. II. Series.

E301.M39 2009
973.3—dc22

2009003679

Chelsea House books are available at special discounts when purchased in bulk quantities for businesses, associations, institutions, or sales promotions. Please call our Special Sales Department in New York at (212) 967-8800 or (800) 322-8755.

You can find Chelsea House on the World Wide Web at http://www.chelseahouse.com

The Discovering U.S. History series was produced for Chelsea House by Bender Richardson White, Uxbridge, UK

Editors: Lionel Bender and Susan Malyan
Designer and Picture Researcher: Ben White
Production: Kim Richardson
Maps and graphics: Stefan Chabluk
Cover printed by Bang Printing, Brainerd, MN
Book printed and bound by Bang Printing, Brainerd, MN
Date printed: April 2010
Printed in the United States of America

10 9 8 7 6 5 4 3 2 1

This book is printed on acid-free paper.

All links and web addresses were checked and verified to be correct at the time of publication. Because of the dynamic nature of the web, some addresses and links may have changed since publication and may no longer be valid.

Contents

Introduction

Exploring the West

During the 1780s and 1790s few Americans even imagined that the huge tract of land known as Louisiana might become U.S. territory. However, as European politics and wars played themselves out in North America and Europe, that vast region slipped out from under Spanish control to French ownership at the turn of the century. Then, much to the surprise of Americans, especially President Thomas Jefferson, France offered to sell the whole of Louisiana to the United States. This purchase more than doubled the size of the United States and its western reach. It was the greatest land deal in U.S. history.

The acquisition of Louisiana in 1803 made one thing clear: America's reach exceeded its grasp. The United States had purchased a region that almost no one in the country knew anything about. Jefferson therefore decided to send a party of American explorers out to these Far Western lands to report details of the mysterious region, including weather patterns, animals, plant life, minerals, and the geology and topography of the land. He also wanted the expedition to form friendships with the Indians in hopes of profiting from the great western fur trade with the native Americans. Jefferson tapped Meriwether Lewis to lead the expedition and Lewis brought on William Clark to serve as co-captain.

THE EXPEDITION SETS OUT

Lewis and Clark formed a "Corps of Discovery" of skilled hunters, rivermen, blacksmiths, tanners, carpenters, and soldiers. A total of 45 men set out from near St. Louis on the afternoon of May 14, 1804, at 4 o'clock. The great, rolling Missouri River would be their watery highway into the West. Yet, at the opening of the nineteenth century the Missouri was an untamed and uncontrollable waterway, where sandbars and trees that had fallen into the water constantly threatened to rip the bottoms out of boats. Across the territory of the modern-day state of Missouri, the river was flanked by limestone bluffs. Lewis often walked along the banks, searching for new plant life and anything else of note.

As summer moved into fall the Corps of Discovery continued up the Missouri River, reaching the lands of the Louisiana Territory that are today Nebraska, Iowa, North Dakota, and South Dakota. At every stage Lewis recorded scientific data, while Clark worked on a detailed map. Both captains, along with a handful of other men, kept journals and personal diaries of everything they encountered. When they saw a new animal, they often drew a picture of it or even tried to capture one.

PEOPLES OF THE GREAT PLAINS

In late July the expedition reached the lands of the Missouri and Otoe Indians, at a site some 20 miles (32 kilometers) north of today's Omaha, Nebraska. They offered gifts to the

Indians and tried to explain that these native peoples of the Great Plains now had a new father, one who lived far off to the East—President Jefferson. The site became known to Americans as Council Bluffs.

As they made further progress along the river, the Americans met other Plains nations, including the Yankton Sioux near today's Yankton, South Dakota, and their neighbors, the Teton Sioux outside the modern-day capital of South Dakota, Pierre. During that late September encounter, Teton warriors tried to take one of the expedition's pirogues (canoes). This resulted in a face-off, with hundreds of Sioux aiming their arrows at the members of the Corps while the Americans aimed their rifles and the cannon on the keelboat at the Indians. Fortunately, the tense moment ended peacefully.

The party progressed further up the Missouri, where they met the Arikara people near the mouth of the Grand River, then the Mandan and Hidatsa, who were living together in several villages north of today's Bismarck, North Dakota. It was now October and Lewis and Clark chose to spend the Corps' first winter with these friendly Indians. During the months spent encamped with the Mandan and Hidatsa the men experienced bitter cold, with the thermometer dropping to −50° F (−46° C). The Missouri froze over, allowing the Americans and Indians to cross from village to fort. These were peaceful days spent with Indians who were hospitable, always willing to trade American tools for baskets of corn.

The Mandan villages were the last point on the Missouri River generally known to Americans. Come spring the Corps of Discovery would be crossing completely unknown territory. That winter they gained information from the Indians about a great waterfall to the west. They also hired a French fur trapper, named Toussaint Charbonneau, who agreed to take the Americans upriver. With him was his 15-year-old Shoshone wife, named Sacajawea. Her people lived further west and it

Meriwether Lewis on the expedition, wearing a fur hat and snakeskins. Prior to setting out, under Jefferson's instructions, Lewis studied medicine, mapmaking, navigating, botany, and Indian history.

became a goal for the party to make contact with this western nation, who might be able to provide them with horses to make their crossing over the Rocky Mountains.

TO THE WEST

With the arrival of the 1805 spring, the party set out again. Those men with one-year contracts turned back to St. Louis, carrying with them the specimens collected by Lewis. The party was down from more than 45 men to an expedition of 31, plus Sacajawea and her two-month-old son, Pompey. Between the two groups, one heading back downstream and the other continuing upstream, most would never see one another again.

Captain Lewis was so struck by the landscape around him that he wrote in his journal: "This immense river waters one of the fairest portions of the globe. Nor do I believe that there is in the universe a similar extent of country. As we passed on, it seemed as if those scenes of visionary enchantment would never have an end."

On July 22 the men reached the site known today as the Three Forks of the Missouri River, where three streams form the headwaters of the great western river. Now they knew the Missouri did not flow to the Pacific Ocean. The party soon met the Shoshone people, who lived in the Bitterroot Range of the Rockies. Their initial encounter was tentative, with the Indians uncertain about who this well-armed party of men, accompanied by a woman and a baby, might be. In a twist of fortune and fate Sacajawea recognized the leader of the Shoshone band—he was Cameahwait, her brother! This guaranteed the Americans would receive the horses they needed.

In late August the Corps of Discovery began their ascent into the highest elevations of the Rocky Mountains. This leg of the trip proved one of the most challenging they would face. Snows fell at night, covering the men. They lost their way. The men began a starvation march, reduced to eating the horses and even their candles. Finally, they crossed the Continental Divide, the great spine of the Rockies, and began their descent toward western-flowing rivers, including the Clearwater, the Snake, and the Columbia. Along the way they encountered more Indians, including the Nez Perce, most of whom had never seen white men or guns before. After hacking out new dugout canoes, the expedition pushed on, struggling through dangerous rapids, down to the Pacific Coast. For the first time they were finally paddling downriver. At the mouth of the Columbia they built a garrison called Fort Clatsop, where they spent a miserable winter.

HOMEWARD BOUND

By the following spring of 1806 everyone in the party was homesick and ready to return to the United States. They had been gone for so long that many Americans back East thought the party must have perished. On the journey back, a confident Lewis and Clark split the expedition into five separate parties to enable them to cover more territory. While exploring the Marias River with a handful of men, Lewis had a violent encounter with several Blackfeet warriors, who tried to steal their horses and guns at night. During the fight, two Blackfeet were killed, one by Lewis, retaliating at a man who had just shot him. Other than Sergeant Floyd, a member of the party who died of appendicitis in August 1804, these were the only casualties of the Lewis and Clark expedition.

By August all the members of the expedition were back together, headed toward the Mandan villages and a joyous reunion. After spending some time with their Indian friends, the Americans returned to the Missouri River, and set out for St. Louis. While the trip up the Missouri to the Mandan encampments had taken five months back in 1804, their trip downriver in 1806 only took five weeks! On September 23 they reached St. Louis, and the whole town came out to celebrate.

On the expedition Lewis and Clark had catalogued 178 plants and 122 animals previously unknown to American and European scientists. Clark had produced a map so accurate that, of the thousands of miles the party had covered, he was only off by 40 miles (64 kilometers)! The party had met with 58 different tribes of Indians and had only experienced one violent encounter, that with the Blackfeet. They had crisscrossed thousands of miles of the West, helping to solidify their nation's claim to a vast territory and ensuring that, one day, not too many decades in the future, the United States would stretch from the Atlantic to the Pacific Ocean.

Yet the lands west of the Mississippi River still seemed remote to most Americans. Even Jefferson, who had dispatched Lewis and Clark to explore the trackless western wilderness, could not imagine an expanded America that spread all the way to the Rockies. He even suggested that it would take Americans a hundred generations to fill in the west of the Louisiana Territory. The president could not have been more wrong. Americans were to accomplish that monumental feat in less than four generations.

States and Territories

This map shows that, by 1850, the nation spread from the Atlantic Ocean to the Pacific Ocean and was complete except for Alaska, Hawaii, and parts of the southwest. Most of the mainland was divided into territories. Westward trails led from east of the Mississippi River to Oregon Country.

PACIFIC OCEAN

MEXICO

0   500 Miles

0   500 Kilometers

ALASKA

N

0   500 Miles

0   500 Kilometers

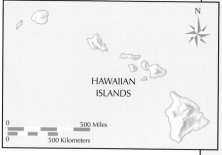

N

HAWAIIAN ISLANDS

0   500 Miles

0   500 Kilometers

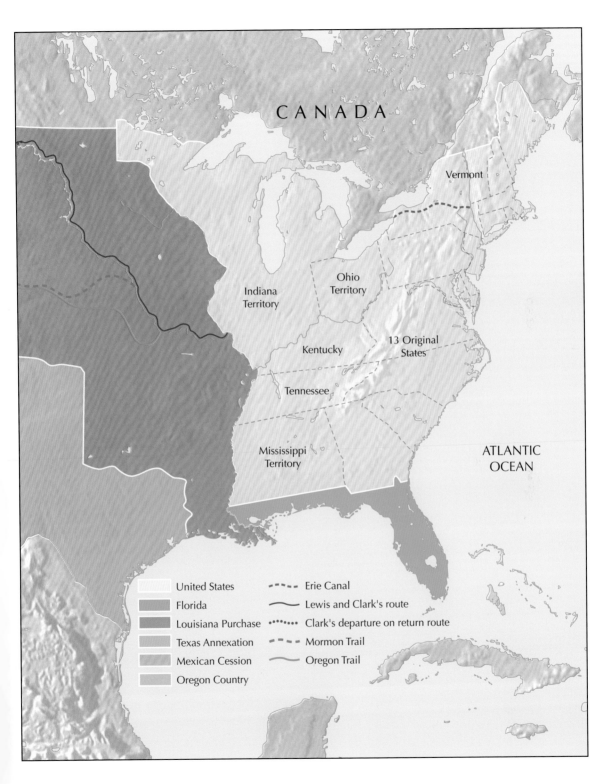

CANADA

Vermont

Ohio
Territory

Indiana
Territory

Kentucky

13 Original
States

Tennessee

Mississippi
Territory

ATLANTIC
OCEAN

United States
Florida
Louisiana Purchase
Texas Annexation
Mexican Cession
Oregon Country

- - - - Erie Canal
———— Lewis and Clark's route
•••••• Clark's departure on return route
- - - Mormon Trail
———— Oregon Trail

1

The New Nation Takes Shape

After struggling with a constitution that limited the power of the national government, while granting too much power to the various states, a new constitution was framed in Philadelphia during the long, hot summer of 1787. Eleven states had ratified the document by July 1788. The old constitution—the Articles of Confederation—was dead, and the new constitution was the law of the land. During the debates over establishing a new constitution, some critics had complained that it did not include a list of the rights of each American citizen. This was a problem that would have to be addressed, and soon.

The new American government included a Senate and House of Representatives, as well as a national court system, and an executive branch. Electors were selected from each state and, on the first Wednesday of January 1789, those electors chose the nation's first president and vice president. Until the ratification of the Twelfth Amendment in 1804, each elector held two votes and the two top vote recipients became president and vice president, respectively.

THE FIRST PRESIDENT

There was never any question about who the first president might be. Virginian George Washington had served his country during the years of revolution and war, as a delegate to the Continental Congress, as the commander in chief of the Continental Army, and as the president of the Constitutional Convention in Philadelphia. He was chosen unanimously. John Adams from Massachusetts was selected as his vice president. These two executive leaders represented both the North and South of the young republic. The process of selecting them had nothing to do with political parties as they exist today, for such parties had not yet been formally established.

Over the six months following Washington's inauguration, the new federal government may have been as productive as it has been ever since. The new Congress raised some much needed revenue with the passage of the Tonnage Act of 1789, which created customs duties on imports on a sliding scale. The new legislature also created three executive departments to serve Washington—State, Treasury, and War. Washington made the first appoints which included Thomas Jefferson as Secretary of State, Alexander Hamilton over the Treasury Department, and Henry Knox, who had served as a general under Washington, as Secretary of War.

Congress, empowered by the new Constitution, created a federal system of courts and judges by approving the Judiciary Act of 1789. The highest court created was the U.S. Supreme Court, with six justices, including the first Chief Justice, John Jay. There were three circuit courts of appeal, and a district court for each state. The act also created the office of Attorney General. Congress additionally passed a

A portrait of George Washington (1732–1799) as president. At his inauguration on April 30, he took the oath of office, promising to "preserve, protect, and defend the Constitution of the United States."

Bill of Rights to be added as amendments to the Constitution. Those amendments were not ratified, or accepted, by the states until December 1791.

WASHINGTON'S MONEY ISSUES

When Washington took the reins of the presidency, his Secretary of the Treasury, 34-year-old Alexander Hamilton, immediately suggested bold steps to help put the government on a sound financial footing. Through a series of reports to Congress between January 1790 and December 1791, he suggested that the national debt—a whopping $54 million—should be paid off at face value. He also proposed that the federal government should take over (his word was "assume") close to $25 million of state debts, most of which had been run up to support the Revolutionary War effort. Since most southern states had already paid their debts, their representatives, including James Madison, were none too keen on Hamilton's proposal. A compromise was soon in the making.

In June 1790 Thomas Jefferson hosted a dinner party, to which he invited Madison and Hamilton. The three Founding Fathers sat down together and worked out an arrangement: Madison agreed not to fight Hamilton's proposal in the House if Hamilton agreed to move the federal capital to the banks of the Potomac River, the boundary between the southern states of Virginia and Maryland. Hamilton agreed. The Compromise of 1790 resulted in the establishment of a new capital by the following month, although the government did not take up residence at this new location immediately. Pennsylvania did not support the compromise until Congress agreed to move the capital to Philadelphia during the decade that the new government buildings were under construction.

Hamilton issued other economic reports, calling for the establishment of a national bank and a national mint; the creation of excise, or internal, taxes on distilled spirits; and government aid and encouragement in the development of manufacturing and factories. His bank proposal raised much criticism, again from Madison, who believed that such a bank was unconstitutional, as this institution was not mentioned in the Constitution. But Congress passed the bill in early 1791, its supporters citing the section of the Constitution that allows Congress to pass "all laws necessary and proper" to carry out its powers. Their logic was clear: How can the Congress implement funding for assumption and tax laws and western land sales without a place to put government funds that was connected, in some way, to the federal government?

Against Jefferson's and Madison's wishes, Hamilton's proposals became reality. The new bank was capitalized at $10 million, with only 20 percent of the deposits coming from public, or government, funds.

The Whiskey Rebellion

As controversial as the bank issue was with such men as Jefferson and Madison, this was nothing compared to the controversy caused by the new excise tax on alcohol, which provoked widespread anger. The tax was passed on March 3, 1791, and almost immediately farmers who produced whiskey and other spirits in country stills, especially in western Pennsylvania, protested against it. There, farmers regularly processed their grain into moonshine and sold it to eastern markets, including Philadelphia. The farmers not only refused to pay the tax, they attacked the federal revenue agents who tried to collect it. Fearful of a rebellion, President Washington ordered all the western whiskey rebels to, as noted by historian James Thomas Flexner, "disperse and retire peaceably to their homes" before September 1. To show how serious he was, he ordered up 13,000 militiamen to march into western Pennsylvania if needed. But the "Whiskey Rebellion" was short-lived and, at the sight of troops, the country distillers evaporated like so much alcohol.

POLITICAL PARTIES AND CRISES

Hamilton's establishing of a national bank and assumption of the public debt were interpretations of the scope of the Constitution, and caused a divide to develop between him and his fellow cabinet member Thomas Jefferson. Hamilton's view of the Constitution was that the document was flexible and that the government had powers that might not be expressly stated in the pages of the Constitution. He saw a future America as a place that would be increasingly urbanized, its economy diversified, and where the landscape would be dotted with factories, mills, and foundries. The New Yorker also felt that political decisions should be entrusted to a strong central government, supported by weaker state powers, with well-educated, leading citizens at the top.

Jefferson, on the other hand, was a strict interpreter of the Constitution. He believed in an American system that was based on farming, and intelligent, common men capable of making democratic decisions. The result was, by 1797, two rival political parties—Hamilton's Federalists and Jefferson's Republicans or Republican Democrats. (The reader should not confuse today's Republican or Democrat Parties with Jefferson's party.)

Not only did these two Founding Fathers split over their domestic political views, they also disagreed on which foreign power the United States should principally ally itself with. Hamilton was pro-British, while Jefferson was a Francophile—he loved the French. When France exploded into revolution against its own monarchy in 1789, Jefferson wanted Washington to lend U.S. support to the French, especially when various European powers—including Britain—went to war with France to halt its destructive revolution. Hamilton, naturally, wanted to support the British. President Washington soon faced a dilemma. Many other Americans were also calling for him to support one or the other side. Wisely, Washington chose to keep the United States out of the widespread European conflict by issuing a Proclamation of Neutrality on April 22, 1793. He urged Americans to remain personally neutral as well.

Mixed Reactions, Confused Situations

Washington could not simply ignore either European power, however, especially Great Britain. The British had never fully evacuated their forts in the old northwest region around the Great Lakes, despite their agreement to do so under the Treaty of 1783, and they were rumored to be arming Indians in the region against the Americans. In addition, both British and French naval ships were regularly attacking American merchant vessels on the high seas, confiscating any cargoes bound for the other nation.

To find solutions to such problems, Washington sent the Supreme Court Chief Justice, John Jay, to London in 1794 with a mission to conclude another treaty with England. Jay managed to get a treaty, although it was somewhat unfavorable to the United States. The treaty was, perhaps, better than no treaty, and it did bring 10 years of peace and prosperity in a world torn by major war, but many Americans were dissatisfied with Jay's accomplishment.

Jay's Treaty had immediate results. It further established the divide between the Federalists and Republican Democrats. John Jay was vilified, and angry mobs hanged him in effigy. Even Washington was criticized, and at one Virginia dinner party a toast was made calling for his immediate death. According to the historian Robert Remini, Jefferson was negative about the treaty, referring to Washington as the

"Samson whose head was shaved by that Harlot England."
The criticism was so harsh that Washington chose not to run
for a third term as president.

In 1795, however, the Washington administration negotiated another treaty, which proved extremely popular. An
American negotiator, Southerner Thomas Pinckney, managed
to bring about an agreement with Spain, called the Treaty of
San Lorenzo (many Americans simply called it Pinckney's
Treaty). The Spanish were in control of the Louisiana Territory and the port of New Orleans. Americans living in the
Trans-Appalachian West were increasingly reliant on using
this port to sell their farm produce and feared that the Spanish might one day cut off the port to Americans. Pinckney's
Treaty guaranteed Americans the right to ship their produce
down the Mississippi and to export their goods, without pay-
ing a customs duty, out of New Orleans. For the moment,
the West appeared safe from having the port of New Orleans
closed to its inhabitants.

THE NEXT PRESIDENT IS CHOSEN

With Washington's decision to leave the presidency, the
election of 1796 was an open race. The Federalists selected
Vice President John Adams as their presidential candidate,
and the Republicans chose the obvious Thomas Jefferson.
Unlike the previous two elections, both candidates ran with
running mates: men who intended to serve as vice president.
Since electors cast two ballots each, the parties were hoping
that each elector would vote once for a presidential candidate and then use his second vote for the vice presidential
running mate.

Adams's fellow Federalist was Thomas Pinckney, the
South Carolinian who had negotiated the treaty with Spain,
while the Republicans tapped a New Yorker and Revolutionary War veteran, Aaron Burr. While the candidates did not

actively run for office, their parties ran them, hosting mass rallies and bonfires, barbecues and stump speeches, and producing printed posters and handbills.

Adams and the Federalists received support from New Englanders, including those involved in shipping, banking, manufacturing, and other commercial interests. Jefferson's supporters were fellow Southerners, small merchants and craftsmen, as well as a host of small-time farmers. In the end Adams won the electoral vote by 71 to 68 over Jefferson. However, the Constitution at that time still required the runner-up to take the office of vice president, regardless of his party, so Jefferson the Republican became vice president to Federalist president Adams.

ADAMS AS CHIEF EXECUTIVE

John Adams was 61 years old when he took office as president in the spring of 1797. One of the most important of the Founding Fathers, Adams was highly intelligent, but extremely egotistical, a man of principle and virtue, but stubborn and willful.

A pair of major events marked John Adams's single term of office. The first occurred when American diplomats tried to sit down and negotiate with the revolutionary French government in 1797. They were told no such talks could begin until they had paid a bribe of $250,000. The diplomats refused, word was sent back to the States, and soon Americans responded angrily. The scandal became known as the "XYZ Affair," the code names given to the three French agents with whom the American diplomats met. The result was an undeclared naval war with the French, sometimes called the Quasi War, during which ships of both nations attacked each other on the high seas. The conflict lasted for two years, until 1800. With no navy available, Congress created the Department of the Navy and commissioned the construction of a small handful of sleek frigates. At the same time, Congress increased the size of the U.S. Army to 20,000 men, plus 30,000 reserve forces. Through the winter of 1798, 14 American ships were fitted for naval service, plus 200 armed merchant ships.

The second event was focused more at home. Fearing that the Republican Party—which tended to be supportive of the French and their violent revolution—might also be influenced by them at home, the Federalists in Congress passed a number of laws designed to combat plots that might involve Americans (read "Republicans") acting against the U.S. government. The Alien and Sedition Acts, passed in June and July 1798, respectively, placed serious restrictions on both American citizens and on immigrants from Europe. One of the acts, the Naturalization Act, increased the number of years an alien would have to wait before becoming a citizen from 5 to 14 years. The Alien and Alien Enemies Act empowered the president to deport or jail anyone he considered a threat to the United States and its peace and safety. The Sedition Act threatened citizens and aliens alike with imprisonment for publishing any "false, scandalous and malicious writing" about the U.S. government, Congress, or the president. Fortunately, the Naturalization and Sedition acts had a short shelf life, and were repealed or expired between 1800 and 1802. The Alien Enemies Act is still in force today and was used in World Wars I and II.

These Federalist-inspired acts took such bold steps to trample on the personal liberties of even American citizens that Jefferson and Madison responded by writing a set of resolutions, which were passed by the Kentucky and Virginia legislatures in 1798. The Kentucky and Virginia Resolutions argued that the Alien and Sedition Acts were unconstitutional. The authors even suggested that state legislatures had the power to "nullify," or declare void and non-binding, these laws in their states. Jefferson and Madison also argued a state could even secede from the United States as a solution to their dissatisfaction with federal laws it deemed unconstitutional. These issues of nullification and secession would continue into the nineteenth century, eventually taking root in the events leading up to the American Civil War.

A NEW CAPITAL CITY

During his last year as president Adams signed the bill that ordered the federal government's capital to move to its new location along the banks of the Potomac River. In June 1800 Adams made his first trip to the new capital, where he found an unfinished series of government buildings, including his new presidential home, the Executive Mansion. In November, the Sixth Congress took up business in the new Federal City, later known as Washington City, after the former president whose Mount Vernon estate was only a few miles away. (Washington had died in 1799.) Once convened, the new Congress was immediately faced with a thorny political problem—choosing the new president.

President Adams ran for a second term as a Federalist, this time with Charles Cotesworth Pinckney, brother of Thomas Pinckney, as his running mate. Again, Jefferson ran against him for the presidency, with Aaron Burr for Republican vice president. The Republican candidates were chosen by a new method, a caucus, or closed meeting, held by the party. This remained the method of nominating candidates until 1824, when it failed to reach a decision and was replaced by state legislatures making the choice, and later, in 1832, by party conventions with delegates representing every state. This remains the practice today.

The most damaging impact on Adams's run for reelection came from within his own party of Federalists. Alexander Hamilton, who despised how Adams had conducted himself during his first term, campaigned against him. Hamilton's action was decisive. The result was that Adams received 65 votes while Jefferson took 73.

JEFFERSON AS PRESIDENT

On March 4, 1801, Virginian Thomas Jefferson became the first president to be inaugurated in the new capital, Federal City. He walked that morning from his lodgings the two blocks to the still unfinished Capitol building and took the oath of office in the Senate Chamber, from Chief Justice John Marshall, who had replaced John Jay. Jefferson delivered his inaugural address, then walked back to his boarding house,

THE FEDERALISTS AND AARON BURR

President Thomas Jefferson had reason to enjoy his first term as president of the United States. However, his successes led envious Federalists to take desperate measures to regain some of the political power they had lost due to Jefferson's and the Republicans' popularity.

The Federalist plan, cooked up in Congress, called for the establishment of a new "confederacy," one separate from the Southern States. They called it the "Northern Confederacy," and it was to include New Jersey, New York, New England, and even Canada, if possible. The group of schemers approached Vice President Aaron Burr to support their plans. Burr was already angry over losing the presidency to Jefferson, following a tied electoral college vote. He said yes to their offer, in return for Federalist support for his bid for the governorship of New York.

The scheme never played itself out, however, and Burr ran into trouble himself when, in 1804, he shot Alexander Hamilton in a duel. Facing a murder indictment, Burr fled south, hiding out in Georgia, then South Carolina. Eventually, the indictment was thrown out, and Burr was allowed to finish his term as vice president.

where he ate dinner at the same table as the other guests. As president, Jefferson proved to be a simple man, despite his sometimes elegant tastes, which included French wines. He did not like much pomp and circumstance. He discarded the coach and six horses that Washington had used while president, and shook hands with people, where Washington had only bowed.

Jefferson's first term as president went fairly well. In his inaugural address, he had called on both political parties to put their differences aside: "We are all Republicans; we are all Federalists. If there be any among us who would wish to dissolve the Union or change its republican form, let them

But Burr's days of conspiracy were not over. His political fortunes having been used up in the East, in 1805 he went west to St. Louis. There he met up with an old friend, U.S. Army General James Wilkinson, then the military governor of Louisiana. The two men hatched a scheme, which appears to have involved Burr establishing a western nation around himself, perhaps in the Mississippi Valley or even in Spanish-held territory, such as California, modern-day Texas, or New Mexico. Burr and 60 co-conspirators even made a trip down the Mississippi to New Orleans, where they intended to seize the city from U.S. control. But before Burr and his men could pull off their plot, Wilkinson betrayed him, informing Jefferson of the conspiracy. When Burr received word of this, he called off his plans.

The U.S. government soon placed a reward of $2,000 for Burr's capture. When Burr tried to flee, he was caught in Mississippi Territory. He was taken to Richmond, Virginia, where he was placed on trial for treason. Ultimately he was found innocent of the charges, since he had never made an actual attempt to seize American territory. However, the infamous case, along with the former vice president's ties to the earlier plot, was unpopular with the general public and did not help the future of the Federalist Party in America.

stand undisturbed as monuments of the safety with which error of opinion may be tolerated where reason is left free to combat it." Jefferson was noting a subtle, but important, step the nation had taken. The American people had just witnessed the transfer of power from one party to another, without bloodshed, civil war, conspiracy, or scandal.

But there were still party differences and antagonisms. Almost immediately upon taking office, Jefferson had to deal with a party confrontation left for him by outgoing President Adams. (Several years earlier, Jefferson and Adams, once friends, had experienced a falling out over politics. Their personal relationship would not be rekindled until years later, when both had gone into retirement.) As the Federalists had lost the presidency and control of the Congress, they tried to prop up their political power by appointing new Federalist judges under the recently created Judiciary Act. The president was still signing off on these appointments through the last day of his term, giving rise to the term "Midnight Appointees." Jefferson refused to recognize many of these appointments, and supported the repeal of the Judiciary Act of 1801 the following year.

FOREIGN CHALLENGES AND SUCCESSES

Among the successes of Jefferson's first term was the purchase of the Louisiana Territory from the French leader, Napoleon Bonaparte. When the Spanish closed the port of New Orleans to American trade traffic in October 1802, Jefferson moved quickly. Historian Remini notes the importance New Orleans represented to the young republic and its president, who said: "There is on the globe one single spot the possessor of which is our natural and habitual enemy. It is New Orleans." The president dispatched to France the former American ambassador to France, James Monroe, where he was to help Robert Livingston of New York in negotiating an agreement with the French. Jefferson had authorized his diplomatic pair to offer $10 million to purchase New Orleans and West Florida, even though Congress had only authorized $2 million. In the meantime, Congress agreed a call-up of 80,000 American militiamen. If the Americans could not make a deal with Napoleon, they would march on New Orleans.

But a deal came easily once Monroe arrived in Paris. Napoleon was ready to sell not only New Orleans, but the whole

A view of New Orleans in 1803, with a banner held by the American eagle stating "Under My Wings, Everything Prospers." The oil painting celebrated Jefferson's Louisana Purchase from the French.

of Louisiana. Yet when the French ministers set the price for Louisiana at $15 million, neither Livingston or Monroe knew exactly what to do—they had not been authorized to spend that amount of money, and they had not been given instructions to purchase the entire region of Louisiana. Feeling it better to accept the offer, rather than let the opportunity drift away, the two envoys agreed, signing a treaty dated April 30, 1803.

When the document reached Jefferson on July 14, the president was also unsure of how to respond. The Constitution did not authorize the acquisition of land, but Jefferson convinced himself of its appropriateness, noting that he had the power to make treaties with foreign powers. There was some wrangling in the Senate among Federalists who were against the purchase, including one who complained, according to historian Thomas Fleming: "We are to give money of which we have too little for land of which we already have too much." But the wise saw the importance of the purchase, including Federalist Alexander Hamilton, Jefferson's old rival, who believed the vast region of Louisiana was vital to the future development of the United States.

2
The War of 1812

In 1803, at the same time that Emperor Napoleon was offering Louisiana to the United States, France went to war with Great Britain—again. Other European powers including Austria, Russia, and Sweden allied with the British, and the conflict spread across Europe. This war would continue for the next 12 years, and always at the center of the conflict was the struggle between France and Great Britain.

OVERSEAS CHALLENGES

The war proved to be good for the Americans, for it provided opportunities for American shippers, traders, and merchants to make high profits from both Britain and France, as well as other European nations involved in the war. Regardless of the politics of the conflict, U.S. businessmen sold to both sides. John Adams said, as noted by historian David Brion Davis, that American merchants and shippers "lined their pockets while Europeans slit each other's throats."

During the years following 1803 and the opening of yet another Napoleonic War, American ships lined European docks, taking high profits home with them. Trade was so good that the wages paid to sailors on U.S. merchant vessels skyrocketed from $8 a month to around $25. This attracted foreign sailors, including former British sailors who willingly surrendered their citizenship and became American citizens. In a few short years, according to historian Richard Kluger, an "estimated 25 percent of the 70,000 or so crewmen in the American commercial fleet were ex-Britons."

Trading with two nations at war with one another proved to be a dangerous game. Both the French and the British seized ships of neutral states found trading with their enemy. The United States, through its neutral trade, had made enemies of both countries. During 1807, the French seized 500 American merchant vessels in international waters. The British captured twice as many.

Forced Service

Over the next few years, American ships remained extremely vulnerable. The British navy often violated the rights of Americans by engaging in a longstanding practice called impressment. To fill a ship's ranks, British naval officers sometimes ordered their sailors to go ashore in ports and kidnap men to serve on board. The British "impressed" men so often that, by 1811, nearly 10,000 American sailors had been forced into service in the British navy.

During the summer of 1807 the Americans experienced one of the most blatant examples of impressment at the hands of the British when an American naval frigate was blindsided by a British man-of-war, the *Leopard*, just 5 miles (8 kilometers) off the American coast. The attack resulted in the killing and wounding of 20 Americans and the capture of four.

Impressment included seizing deserters from British ships in American ports. In search of better living conditions and wages, many British sailors deserted and went to work on American merchant ships.

Trade Embargoes

Word of the attack spread quickly, and Americans everywhere were outraged. There was talk that Americans might soon be pushed into another war with Great Britain. Such a conflict would likely prove disastrous for the United States, President Jefferson thought. The American navy, after all, was miniscule. In contrast, the British navy was the largest on earth.

Jefferson did not pursue war, but engaged in economic tactics instead. He knew how well boycotts of British imports had worked during the American Revolution and decided to implement trade boycotts, called embargoes, again. In December, Jefferson convinced Congress to pass one of his latest proposals, the Embargo Act, which proved disastrous. New England exports fell by 75 percent, and exports from southern ports fell by 85 percent. Three out of four (30,000 of 40,000) American sailors were put out of work. Grass grew on American docks, businesses closed across the country, and, in New York City, 1,200 men were thrown into debtors' prison. Farm prices dropped by 50 percent. President Jefferson found himself playing the same role that the British authorities had during the days of the American Revolution, sending American customs agents out to catch American smugglers.

In the midst of pushing for trade restrictions and embargoes against France and Britain, President Jefferson came to a new realization, one that somewhat altered his view of America's future. He had always thought of the American Republic as an agrarian world, with farm produce providing the backbone of the nation's economy. But with American overseas trade having, in Jefferson's words, "kept us in hot water from the commencement of our government," as noted by historian A. J. Langguth, the Republican president came to the conclusion that America needed to become more self-sufficient. To do so, Jefferson knew, would mean accepting Hamilton's earlier view of an American future increasingly reliant on manufacturing and small factories.

Over the following two years, though, the United States and Great Britain continued to drift toward war. None of the many trade acts passed by Congress seemed to have any effect on either France or Britain. However, what the Americans did not know at the time was that, by the summer of 1812, Great Britain was preparing to alter its policies toward American shipping rights. By cutting off British importations, the Americans had unknowingly pushed Britain's exports so low as to cause an economic depression there. On June 16 the British reopened the Atlantic to uninterrupted shipping for American merchant ships. But the move came too late. Just two days earlier, the United States Congress, at the request of the new President, James Madison, had voted to declare war on Britain.

OPENING THE WAR

When Madison presented his case for war to Congress, he focused almost exclusively on issues related to America's rights on the high seas—British impressments of sailors, blockades of American ports, interference with trade. Yet Congressmen voted in favor of the war for various other reasons. Some wanted to expand the boundaries of the U.S. by, possibly, annexing Canada. Others were interested in fighting the British for the last time, a sort of second war for American independence. Some of those who dreamed of an American Canada were soon labeled as the War Hawks. They included Representative Henry Clay of Kentucky and a southern Representative from South Carolina, John C. Calhoun—young, fiery men who were just beginning to have an impact on American history, but one that would continue over the next 30 years.

Perhaps ironically, despite Madison's call to fight for sea rights, many Easterners did not vote for the war. In the House, representatives from the New England states, plus New York and New Jersey, voted against war by 34 to 14. Westerners and Southerners, however, supported the coming conflict by 65 to 15. In the Senate, the vote for war was close—19 to 13. The majority of nay-sayers were Federalists, who were soon referring to the American–British conflict as "Mr. Madison's War."

Even as the U.S. prepared to go to war, Britain was largely distracted from the conflict by its war with France, which the British Crown considered infinitely more important. But once that war with Napoleon was over, in 1814, the British were able to concentrate entirely on the United States. After two years of fighting, Britain's other hand was no longer tied behind its back. During the early years of the conflict, the U.S. was woefully unprepared to fight. The army was small and ill trained, forcing the government to rely heavily on state militia forces. The American navy was tiny, although it was commanded by a highly trained, experienced officer corps.

FIGHTING ON LAND AND WATER

An American invasion across the Atlantic was absolutely out of the question, so much of the fighting on land took place in North America. Americans had the opportunity to see the war up close. Rather than wait for the British to invade U.S. soil, the Americans invaded Canada, hoping to split alliances between the British and their Indian allies, including those led by a Shawnee chief named Tecumseh.

For the Americans, almost nothing went well. When U.S. General William Hull marched his men toward Detroit, he was roundly defeated by the British, who then gained control of approximately half of the Old Northwest. In fact, Hull surrendered without a fight to a smaller force. Along the second Canadian front, around New York State, the Americans lost the battle of Queenstown on October 13, 1812, near the Niagara River south of Lake Ontario. That fight resulted in the capture of nearly 1,000 American prisoners, including a general and 60 officers. One factor ensuring an American loss occurred when New York militia refused to leave the borders of their state and join the fight on Canadian soil.

The Burning of York

However, the year 1813 did feature some bright spots for the United States. In April American forces advanced on the Canadian town of York (today's Toronto), the capital of Upper Canada, where they engaged the British and overran them inside the town. One of the U.S. officers was Zebulon Pike, whom Jefferson had sent out on an exploration of the upper Mississippi River at the same time that he had sent Lewis and Clark west. At one point in the battle Pike's troops halted close to the town's ammunition dump, which immediately exploded, killing men within 300 yards (275 meters) of the blast. Pike himself was hit and killed. While the British claimed the detonation was an accident, angry Americans subsequently set York on fire, but not until they had pillaged its government buildings and a local church, from which they stole gold and silver plate. In August of the following year the burning of York would lead to a similar action on the part of the British against an American city—Washington City.

Control of the Great Lakes

With the fighting ranging along the Canadian/American border, both sides began to focus their strategies on control of the Great Lakes. Both knew that such control might determine the fate of the Old Northwest. To that end, the British and Americans soon engaged in a boat-building race on Lake Erie. The American efforts were in the hands of 28-year-old Master Commandant Oliver Hazard Perry, who worked alongside a skilled shipbuilder, Noah Brown. In the end, the Americans out built the British, cobbling together ten sleek lake schooners to the Royal Navy's six. These hastily built watercraft engaged one another on September 10, 1813, in the battle of Put-in-Bay. Following a well-timed victory the Americans gained control of the lake and the general vicinity, causing the British to evacuate Detroit. This provided a much-needed boost to American morale.

Just weeks following, General William Henry Harrison (a future president of the United States) was free to sail his 4,500 men, mostly Kentucky volunteers, across Lake Erie to launch a campaign on land. On October 5 Harrison and his men fought and won the battle of the Thames in Canada's Ontario province. During that fight, the Shawnee leader, Tecumseh, was killed. For several years prior to the opening of the war Tecumseh had been rallying his people and other Indian nations in both the Northwest and the Southwest against the Americans, who were encroaching on their lands at an alarming rate. With the Shawnee chief's death, his alliance of tribes fell apart, breaking Indian resistance between the Appalachians and the Mississippi.

Battles at Sea

Yet even as the Americans were winning significant battles in 1813, the British were able to continue dominating the general direction and scope of the conflict. British warships had been patrolling American waters for years prior to the war, and these efforts were stepped up significantly. By the end of 1813, British naval ships were blockading the mouths of Delaware and Chesapeake Bays, to keep American vessels from entering. Most sea-going American trade had been forced into inactivity. By the following year, the blockade included American ports in New England and south to the Gulf of Mexico. The British had a strangulation hold on U.S.

The engagement between USS *Constitution* (on the left) and HMS *Guerriere* (right) on August 19, 1812. Following a fierce exchange of fire, the British ship was sunk.

shipping, cutting off 90 percent of American merchant ships between 1811 and 1814.

However, the United States was not completely incapable of lashing out at the British with its own limited naval resources. Although the American navy only included six actual naval vessels, called frigates, some of these U.S. ships saw victories. The *Constitution* sank a British naval ship, *Guerriere,* off the coast of Canada's Nova Scotia in August 1812, just three days following Hull's surrender at Detroit. Another frigate, the *United States,* under the command of Stephen Decatur, who had, before the war, fought the Barbary Pirates, captured a British warship, *Macedonian,* two months later. In another two months, the *Constitution* sank a second British vessel, the *Java,* off the Brazilian coast. In addition, American citizens, acting as privateers, captured a whopping 450 British merchant vessels, most of them through raids launched from U.S. waters north along the Canadian coast. But for some American naval vessels, the war did not go so well. The *Chesapeake* was defeated in an 1813 battle off the coast of Boston by the British *Shannon.* During that heated engagement, notes historian Ian Toll, the ship's captain, James Lawrence, was killed shortly after he climbed his vessel's rigging and, using a megaphone, shouted down to his crew: "Don't give up the ship!"

FATEFUL 1814

Despite important American victories on land and sea during 1812 and 1813, the war took a decisive turn in Britain's favor in 1814. That spring, Great Britain's war with France ended with the defeat of the French army and the exile of Napoleon to the island of Elba. This left the British free to step up their war efforts against America and redouble their resources. The British military soon launched a major campaign in the region of the Chesapeake Bay. Their primary target was a large masonry military installation in Balti-more—Fort McHenry. But even as the British disembarked on land south of the Maryland port and fort, they chose to first take a detour and march on the U.S. capital of Washington City. It was a last minute decision, apparently made on August 22. That campaign soon brought about one of the most demoralizing defeats the Americans experienced throughout the war.

The British Advance on Washington City

When 4,500 British troops, under the command of General Robert Ross, landed on the Maryland coast, 60 miles (100 kilometers) south of the U.S. capital, they were observed by Secretary of State James Monroe, who watched from a distant hill, surrounded by a small detachment of U.S. cavalry troops known as dragoons. He knew well that Washington City was in jeopardy, but there was little to be done to stop the British advance. In the capital, many citizens were seized with panic, grabbing what belongings they could, and frantically heading north. Officials in Monroe's State Department seized one of the few original copies of the Declaration of Independence, stashed the important founding document into a linen bag, along with other public papers, and hid them in an empty house in Leesburg, Virginia, on the opposite side of the Potomac River.

As the British marched north a few thousand American forces, nearly all militiamen, prepared to make a stand at a spot 18 miles (29 km) south of Washington. On August 23 President Madison rode out to visit them. But later that same day they were called back toward the city, a miserable retreat, the temperature hitting 95°F (35°C). The Americans turned and faced the British in the battle of Bladensburg (Maryland) on August 24, but the militia were easily pushed back. When the American forces arrived in the capital, their commanders ordered them to keep moving, leaving the city open to the advancing British.

As the redcoats approached the American capital, First Lady Dolley Madison was frantically directing servants to remove valuables from the Executive Mansion. She ordered a life-size painting of George Washington by artist Gilbert Stuart to be cut out of its frame and taken. She rescued velvet curtains and other items before being ushered out the rear entrance, into a carriage and whisked across the Potomac into Virginia. Mrs. Madison had no sooner left the city, around 4 P.M., than her husband the president arrived on horseback, along with James Monroe. They did not remain for long, but headed across the bridge to Virginia to catch up with Mrs. Madison.

Washington City is Burned

At 6 P.M., advance guard units of the British army entered the city, ready to seek revenge for the American burning of York in the previous year. They set the Capitol building and the Navy Yard ablaze. They found their way to the Executive Mansion, where British Admiral George Cockburn gathered up souvenirs, including one of Madison's hats and a chair cushion belonging to the First Lady. The British ate food left on a table, broke out all the windows, piled furniture up and burned it, the flames illuminating the night sky.

Washington was on fire. A British soldier later wrote about the scene before him, his words noted by historian Ian Toll:

> *The blazing of houses, ships, and stores, the report of explod-ing magazines, and the crash of falling roofs, informed them (the British) as they proceeded, of what was going forward. It would be difficult to conceive a finer spectacle than that which presented itself as they approached the town. The sky was brilliantly illuminated by the different conflagrations;*

A contemporary colored engraving of the burning of Washington City by British forces on August 24, 1814. The battle raged on the Potomac River as the British continued to fire guns and flares at the city. Buildings caught fire and ammunition stores exploded.

and a dark red light was thrown upon the road, sufficient to permit each man to view distinctly his comrade's face. . . . Of the Senate-House, the President's Palace, the barracks, the dockyard, etc., nothing could be seen except heaps of smoking ruins, and even the bridge, a noble structure upwards of a mile in length, was almost entirely demolished.

There were almost no British casualties as they rampaged through the capital. A dozen men were killed and 50 were injured when one of their comrades tossed a lit torch into a well to extinguish it, not knowing that the well was dry and filled with gunpowder the Americans had hidden from the British. This explosion caused more enemy casualties than musket fire from the town's few defenders.

Fortunately, rain fell later that night, and dampened the fires. However, the storm was accompanied by a tornado that caused further damage to the city. August 24, 1814, had proven to be a day of destruction, humiliation, and defeat for the Americans.

Fort McHenry Stands Firm

But the sideshow of burning Washington City was only a distraction for the British. Their actual goal, Fort McHenry, lay further north. They marched on. One thousand American troops were waiting for the British at the fort. To reach the city of Baltimore, the British would have to sail their ships past McHenry, in the face of its heavy guns. The enemy arrived on September 13, 1814, and commenced firing on the great masonry fortress. Above its ramparts flew an immense American flag specially ordered by Major George Armistead, the fort's commander. This was destined to be remembered as the "Star-Spangled Banner."

The British bombardment of Fort McHenry continued for 25 hours, but their ships were too far away from

THE NATION'S GRAND, OLD FLAG

With the threat of a British invasion against Fort McHenry, Major George Armistead, the fort's commander, made the decision to have a huge battle flag sewn and flown over his fort to stir the patriotism of his men.

A widow and well-known seamstress living in Baltimore, Mary Pickersgill, was chosen to design and sew the grand flag. With the help of her daughter and three nieces, Mary sewed a flag with 15 stars and 15 stripes to represent the 15 states of the union. The flag was enormous. Each stripe measured 2 feet (60 centimeters) across, and each star measured 2 feet (60 cm) from point to point. The stars were sewn onto a blue cloth background. In all, the great American banner measured 42 feet (12.8 meters) long and 30 feet (9.1 m) wide. The flag required 400 yards (366 m) of wool bunting.

The great flag sewn by Mary Pickersgill and her family members withstood the British bombardment of Fort McHenry. However, its story had only just commenced. During the assault on September 13–14 an American lawyer named Francis Scott Key was onboard one of the British ships firing shells at the masonry installation. He watched through the night as Mary Pickersgill's flag continued to fly. He was moved by the sight to pen a poem, which was later titled, "The Star-Spangled Banner." When the words were subsequently put to a common tavern song of the day, the new work became immediately popular with patriotic Americans.

Through the centuries the flag that flew over Fort McHenry became worn, its seams pulling against one another. By the mid-1990s the banner, which had been displayed in the Smithsonian for decades, was taken down for restoration. In November 2008, after more than 10 years of painstaking work by textile restorationists, the Star-Spangled Banner was back on public display in the Smithsonian's newly renovated National Museum of American History. The nation's grand old flag had received a complete cleaning and facelift and was ready to inspire a new generation of young Americans with its age-old story.

the fort to cause significant damage, due to low water levels. After firing between 1,500 and 1,800 cannon balls, the British abandoned their campaign against Baltimore. Only four Americans had been killed and, in the aftermath of the destruction of the capital, the British failure to capture Fort McHenry was reason to celebrate.

THE BATTLE OF NEW ORLEANS

The year 1814 was the last full year of the war. Despite British successes on land and sea, the British government was tiring of the conflict, as Britain had been at war for nearly 20 years with the French. By the summer of that year the Americans and the British had opened peace talks in the city of Ghent, Belgium, with Henry Clay leading the small number of American negotiators.

Even as the British had marched on and burned the U.S. capital, other action was taking place in the Old Southwest, the region that includes today's southern states of Tennessee, Alabama, and Mississippi. Much of the fighting there was between American forces and Indians in the region, some of whom had allied with the British. At the center of much of this Indian fighting was a Tennessee politician and militia general, who had fought in the Revolutionary War as a teenager—47-year-old Andrew Jackson. He was tall and ramrod straight, a self-made, wealthy planter. Jackson had engaged in several duels, and had, since the Revolution, according to historian Sean Wilentz, fostered a "hatred of the British and their empire."

An Interlude at Pensacola

When the war came Jackson had sought recruits to fight not only against the British, but also against Indians. One Jackson recruitment poster sought to stir the emotions of his fellow Americans, as noted by historian A. J. Langguth:

Citizens! Your government has at last yielded to the impulse of the nation... Are we the titled Slaves of George the Third? The military conscripts of Napoleon the great? Or the frozen peasants of the Russian Czar? No—we are the free-born sons of America; the citizens of the only republick (sic) now existing in the world.

Jackson's appeal went on to speculate on a possible American seizure of Canada, calling it "an ambition to rival the exploits of Rome."

As Jackson marched south toward the Gulf Coast in the spring of 1814, the British were organizing a campaign to capture New Orleans and close the Mississippi River to American traffic. Even as Secretary of State James Monroe warned him not to enter Spanish Florida, Jackson marched toward the British base camp in Pensacola. On November 7 Jackson attacked the British at Pensacola as Spanish officials watched. The British evacuated the city only after they had blown up the coastal fortifications, so that Jackson and his men could not occupy them.

Jackson Wins the Day

From Pensacola, the Americans headed back west to defend New Orleans, situated at the mouth of the Mississippi River. On December 1 they entered the city and found few defenses in place. Jackson set up a defense line outside the city with 4,000 men at his front and a reserve of another 1,000, and waited for the British, who had landed to the east with 60 ships and 10,000 men. On the morning of January 7, 1815, enemy forces were spotted, and Jackson's men manned their makeshift barricades. As 5,000 British approached in the early morning hours of January 8, American artillery and riflemen began firing on them. The fight exploded. After a two-hour engagement, the British retreated, abandoning the field of battle. As the smoke of battle cleared, the Americans and their allies saw the field before them and the aftermath of the fight, described by historian Sean Wilentz:

> *Not even the most gruesome scenes of backwoods Indian fighting could prepare them… The British dead and wounded lay in scarlet heaps that stretched out unbroken for as far as a quarter mile. Maimed soldiers crawled and lurched about. Eerily, while the battle smoke cleared off, there was a stirring among the slain soldiers, as dazed redcoats who had used their comrades' bodies as shields arose and surrendered to the Americans.*

Even the hard-edged Jackson was shaken by the carnage: 300 British killed, more than 1,000 wounded, and nearly 500 captured or missing—approximately two of every five men the British had thrown into the battle. On the American side, casualties were only 13 men killed, 39 wounded, and 19 missing. Jackson immediately assessed the significance of the fight that would be remembered as the battle of New Orleans, as noted by historian John Spencer Bassett: "The 8th of January will be ever recollected by the British nation, and always hailed by every true American."

Given British losses, their commanders did not take up the battle again and, within a week of the fighting, the entire British army had packed up and sailed away.

3
The Era of Good Feelings

The battle at the mouth of the Mississippi River was the last of the war and had actually taken place after the war was over. On Christmas Eve, 1814, the American commissioners in Ghent finalized a treaty with the British ending the conflict, three weeks before the fight outside New Orleans took place. The agreement was signed in a Belgium monastery. The Senate ratified the agreement by mid-February 1815 and the war came to an official conclusion. The United States had not won the conflict, but, even more significantly, it had not lost it either. With the victory in New Orleans on everyone's lips, Americans emerged from the conflict proud of their efforts, even if their capital had been destroyed.

The war signified to many an end to problems with Great Britain. Indeed, the war represented a corner turned. In 1817 Great Britain and the United States agreed to demilitarize the Great Lakes through the Rush–Bagot Agreement. The next year Great Britain agreed to allow American fish-ing rights in eastern Canadian waters. Later in 1818 both countries established a clear boundary between the United States and Canada along the 49th parallel between the Rockies and modern-day Minnesota. As for the Oregon Country in the Pacific Northwest, both countries accepted joint occupation. It was a new day for Anglo–American relations and cooperation.

The fighting had produced important symbols of patriotic pride, including the legacy of the frigate *Constitution*, more recently dubbed "Old Ironsides," and the "Star-Spangled Banner" that had flown over Fort McHenry. Indians east of the Mississippi had been largely subdued. As noted by historian Robert V. Remini, the Baltimore newspaper, *Niles Weekly Register*, editorialized: "The last six months is the proudest period in the history of the republic. Who would not be an American? Long live the Republic." Perhaps no American emerged from the conflict with greater pride in his efforts than Andrew Jackson. The war catapulted him onto the national stage as a war hero.

NEW NATIONAL DIRECTIONS

While the United States emerged from the conflict a changed nation, nothing was more changed than the country's political system. The war had never been popular with the Federalists from the beginning. Then, in late 1814, Federalist delegates met in Hartford, Connecticut, to discuss seceding from the Union over the conflict. As the war ended a month later, with the United States undefeated, the Federalists suddenly appeared unpatriotic, even treasonous. They lost support from that point on. The party continued to exist in New England and, perhaps, New York, for a few more years, but it was a dying party. This meant the only viable party following the War of 1812 was Jefferson's old Republican-Democrat Party. Without two significant, strong parties in existence, there was a lack of political conflict. Some referred to this postwar period as the "Era of Good Feelings."

The presidency fell into the hands of James Monroe, who inherited the executive office from James Madison. Monroe was the third Virginian in a row to be elected president: He, Jefferson, and Madison dominated the executive office for nearly a quarter century. In the election of 1816 the only states to cast electoral votes for Rufus King, the capable Federalist nominee, were Massachusetts, Connecticut, and Delaware. The electoral count was 183 to 34 in favor of Monroe. By 1817 three out of four seats in the House of Representatives and the U.S. Senate were held by Republicans. Monroe was elected to a second term in 1820 and faced no significant challenger from the Federalists. His opponent was John Quincy Adams (son of John Adams) who ran as an Independent Republican and received a single electoral vote to Monroe's 231!

Monroe did appoint Adams as his Secretary of State, however, just as Monroe had served in that same cabinet role for President Madison. In 1818 Adams negotiated with the Spanish minister Don Luis de Onis to establish the accurate boundaries of the southwestern portion of the Louisiana Territory, a line the United States shared with Spain. The two diplomats drew a line along the Arkansas and Red Rivers and north to the 42nd parallel, which marked the northern border of Spanish-held territory. This meant the Spanish would no longer lay claim to any territory north of the 42nd parallel, the disputed Oregon Country. These agreements meant Spain had negotiated away its rights to some 250,000 square miles (650,000 square kilometers) of territory.

In 1819 the United States and Spain hammered out yet another agreement—the Transcontinental Treaty—by which Spain ceded Florida's 58,666 square miles (151,945 sq. km) to the United States in exchange for the Treasury's assumption of $5 million in American claims against Spain. The Spanish knew they would have trouble holding onto Florida in the future, as Americans appeared ready to spread out in every direction. As for Adams, he was quick to take the credit for these land deals, his words noted by historian Richard Kluger: "The acknowledgment of a definite line of boundary to [the Pacific Ocean] is a great epoch in our history....[T]he first proposal of it in this negotiation was my own."

The annexation of Florida was an important foreign policy move, since the Seminole Indians in that region had regularly engaged in raids across the border onto U.S. territory. Prior to the deal, President Monroe had dispatched General Jackson, now the commander of the U.S. southern army, to engage the Seminole and put an end to these raids. Jackson was punitive, killing a number of Seminoles and burning down their villages. He also captured two British nationals, whom he accused of aiding the Indians. He ordered one hanged and the other shot by a firing squad. By late spring of 1818, Jackson and his men had swept across Florida, captured the Spanish town of Pensacola, and even placed the Spanish governor in a boat pointed toward Cuba, with Jackson scolding him not to return until he could promise he would keep the Seminole from attacking U.S. territory. Now Florida *was* U.S. territory. Through his Seminole campaigns, Jackson kept his reputation as an Indian fighter before the American people, ensuring his postwar popularity. By 1821, Jackson was selected as Florida's first territorial governor.

The Monroe Doctrine

Later, during Monroe's second term as president, the United States and Great Britain pursued another foreign policy redirection. In 1823 the British approached the United States with a proposal to take a stand together in opposition to further colonialism in the Western Hemisphere. Through the early years of the nineteenth century Spain especially had lost many of its old colonies in the Americas, including Mexico and countries in Central and South America, largely through revolutionary actions. While Secretary of State John Quincy Adams was opposed to a joint foreign policy step with the British, President Monroe agreed to it, after he had consulted with former presidents Jefferson and Madison. He went to Congress to announce a new U.S. foreign policy statement, later known as the Monroe Doctrine. Monroe made it clear that any European power considering future colonizing in the Western Hemisphere had better think twice. As historian Richard Kluger notes, Monroe took a firm stand in his address, stating: "The American continents, by the free and independent condition which they have assumed and maintain, are henceforth not to be considered as subjects for future Colonization by any European Power." Any such colonizing effort would be "viewed as the manifestation of an unfriendly disposition toward the United States." The United States now felt secure enough in its world status to take the leadership stage in the Western Hemisphere.

PROGRESS AT EVERY TURN

Change was the watchword after the War of 1812. Americans had gained a new sense of pride, as well as identity. They did not refer to themselves as readily by their state identity—New Yorker, Virginian, Rhode Islander—but instead as Americans. They had united for the war effort and fought to protect their nation, the Republic of the United States. While some Americans thought of the recent conflict as the Second War for American Independence, their ties with Britain now seemed distant. Americans spoke as Americans, with different regional accents, not as British people did. The days of powdered wigs, silk stockings, and knee pants were gone, replaced by long trousers, neckties, and coats.

There was also a distinctly American literature in the offing. During the generation or so following the War of 1812, writers set their works in American locales and relied on themes close to home. New York writer Washington Irving used his native New York as the backdrop for such stories as *The Legend of Rip Van Winkle* and *The Legend of Sleepy Hollow.* Another New York writer, James Fenimore Cooper, set his romantic novels on the American frontier. His *Leatherstocking* series featured a truly American hero, Natty Bumppo, a frontier rifleman with the nickname "Hawkeye."

Colonial America seemed distant to those living in the early nineteenth century. For one, the United States were no longer 13 in number, but 18 just prior to the War of 1812. Vermont, Kentucky, Tennessee, and Ohio had entered the Union by 1803, and Louisiana nearly a decade later, followed by a six-year-run of new states just prior to, during, and following the Monroe years: Indiana (1816), Mississippi (1817), Illinois (1818), Alabama (1819), Maine (1820), and Missouri (1821), bringing the total number of states to 24.

Some of the great changes and redirections experienced in America after the War of 1812 were embodied in a package of internal improvements and economic policies, called the "American System." This had the support of President Monroe; of Henry Clay, now the Speaker of the House of Representatives after his stint as negotiator in Ghent; and his fellow War Hawk, South Carolina representative John C. Calhoun. The "system" included calls of support for new, higher tariffs to protect America's infant industries; internal improvements such as canals; and a new Bank of the United States (which Congress approved and chartered in 1816) that could oversee a solid currency and credit system.

An expanded age of American manufacturing took off following the War of 1812, with new factories and mills coming on line each year. Prior to 1820 New England and the Middle Atlantic states (including New York and Pennsylvania) were home to just 140 cotton mills. A few years later half a million spindles were humming away, producing thread and yarn in such textile mills. To protect these and other domestic industries, Congress enacted the country's first protective tariff in the spring of 1816. It placed a 25 per-

The Return of Rip Van Winkle—a painting depicting a scene in Washington Irving's book. Irving is regarded as the first American "Man of Letters."

cent duty on imported woolen and cotton goods, as well as a 30 percent duty on imported iron products. The plan was to provide government encouragement of American manufacturing by blocking foreign competition. Slowly, the country was slipping further away from Thomas Jefferson's dream and toward Alexander Hamilton's reality. The United States was growing and expanding in population, as well as geographically. American movement and mobility meant new roads, new bridges, and dozens of new canals.

The Erie Canal

The grandest canal was constructed between 1817 and 1825 in upstate New York: the Erie Canal. When completed, this canal was more than 10 times longer than any previously constructed artificial waterway in America. How it was built is a story of engineering miracles.

The father of the canal was a New York politician who had served as governor of New York state and mayor of New York City—DeWitt Clinton. For years, he had dreamed of a canal across his state, one to connect New York City by water directly to the Great Lakes. But to build a canal across New York was a daunting task. The canal was built 40 feet (12 meters) wide, four feet (1.2 m) deep, and 364 miles (586 km) in length. Since the land covered by the canal rose in elevation by 555 feet (169 m) between Buffalo and Albany, the project amounted to much more than simply digging a long ditch.

The eight-year project included constructing 83 locks— specially designed water chambers used to raise and lower canal boats—along the full length of the canal. There were 27 locks in the 15 miles (24 km) between Albany and Schenectady alone. As for digging the canal itself, this required the labor of thousands of seasonal workers, each paid 50 cents a day. Irish immigrants who worked on the canal might

THE ERIE CANAL

The canal allowed boats to travel in both directions across unequal water levels by closing off sections between lock gates and adding or removing water to change the level. It reduced the transportation time for goods from Lake Erie to New York by up to 60 percent and reduced associated costs by up to 90 percent. Factories and workshops were soon set up along the canal to utilize the new and efficient form of transportation.

1. Lock gates
2. Canal
3. Canal boat
4. Towpath
5. Lockeepers' house
6. Timber freight
7. Canal basin
8. Sawmill
9. Town

be paid just 10 cents a day back home. Thousands of tree stumps had to be pulled out (a task for which canal engineers created a special stump-removing machine pulled by horses), while rock outcroppings blocking the canal's path had to be blasted away. Rock barriers were removed with an

THE MISSOURI COMPROMISE

One dramatic controversy that unfolded during the Monroe administration took place when the Missouri Territory made application to become a new state. Normally, such applications were encouraged, as a sign of the country's progress and further movement west. But there was a fly in the ointment with Missouri, because it sought admission into the Union as a slave state.

In 1819, the year Missouri applied for statehood, the nation was evenly split between slave and free states, with 11 of each. It had become important, even crucial, to both Northerners and Southerners that a balance of power between these two elements be maintained in the U.S. Senate, where neither would have a majority that might allow one section to direct policy over the other. It was a tenuous balance, however, and one that could not be maintained forever.

Five new slave states had already been added to the United States prior to 1820, but they were all in the South—Kentucky, Tennessee, Louisiana, Mississippi, and Alabama. But in Missouri's case the Northerners held firm and refused to accept a new slave state, especially one located in the West. With Missouri's application, the door seemed ready to open on slavery's expansion across the entire western region of the Louisiana Territory, some 800,000 square miles (2 million sq. km) of land. Northerners were convinced that, if slavery were allowed to expand in that region, there would be no limit to its eventual reach. As noted by historian Adrienne Koch, an aged Thomas Jefferson, a slaveholder himself, expressed immediate concern over the possible expansion of slavery into the West, writing in a letter to a friend that the potential explosive called Dupont's Blasting Powder, since dynamite and nitroglycerin had not yet been invented. To make the canal watertight, engineers went out and discovered local deposits of trass, a natural substance that turns rock hard with water exposure.

struck him like "a fire bell in the night, [which] awakened and filled me with terror."

The lines of conflict were laid down in Congress. A New York representative, James Tallmadge, introduced an amendment to limit slavery in Missouri, calling for no new slaves in the new state and freedom for all slave children there at age 25. While the amendment passed the House, it failed in the Senate. Southerners were up in arms, claiming that slavery should not be limited by Congress. Some even talked of seceding from the Union. A Georgia senator, Freeman Walker, as noted by historian Elizabeth Varon, spoke of "civil war... a brother's sword crimsoned with a brother's blood." Northerners observed that Congress had already limited slavery's expansion under the Articles of Confederation. The Northwest Ordinance had established that region as slave-free.

The logjam between Northerners and Southerners came to an end when Kentucky Representative Henry Clay worked out a compromise in 1820. Missouri was allowed to enter as a slave state while Maine came into the Union as a free state, thus maintaining the balance of power in the Senate. But there was another aspect to the compromise. A line was drawn along the southern border of Missouri at the 36 degrees, 30 minutes parallel. Future states carved out of the former Louisiana Territory north of that line would not be opened to slavery. Slavery, even as it might move further west, would remain a "Southerner" institution. For the moment, a true crisis had been averted. But the compromise only postponed the inevitable future clashes over slavery and its expansion. As Thomas Jefferson noted in his letter: "It is hushed, indeed, for the moment. But this is a reprieve only, not a final sentence."

Once completed, the Erie Canal had an immediate effect on the nation's economy. In fact its impact began even before the whole canal was finished, since portions of its length opened as they were completed. Prior to the construction of the canal, a farmer might have paid $100 to have a ton of produce shipped by wagon from Buffalo to New York City, a trip that took three weeks to complete. The farmer could now ship that same ton along that same distance on the Erie Canal (then down the Hudson River) in just one week, at a cost of $5 to $10.

The success of the Erie Canal gave rise to a canal building craze in America. By 1840 more than 4,000 miles (6,450 km) of canals were in operation across the eastern regions of the United States.

A NATION EXPANDING

The Monroe years were marked by expansion in many areas: in population, in movement west, in industrialization, and in the nation's overall economy. After struggling with economic problems prior to and during the early years of the War of 1812, the country enjoyed a run of five prosperous years between 1814 and 1819. Prices were booming for American farmers, who sold their wheat at $2 a bushel and cotton for 30 cents a pound. Southerners moved out of the Old South into the New South, including western Tennessee, Alabama, Mississippi, Louisiana, and even Texas, or *Tejas* as it was known to the Mexicans who controlled it until the successful Texas Revolution of the 1830s. Endless acres of southern land came under cotton cultivation for the first time, as the Bank of the United States extended credit to land speculators and other business promoters. The federal government's income rose sharply as public land sales skyrocketed.

Fueling this great movement across the South and the frenzied expansion of cotton markets in America was a single piece of technology, one that became popular after the turn of the century. During the early 1790s a Northerner named Eli Whitney visited a southern plantation, owned by the widow of former Revolutionary War general Nathaniel Greene. There, Whitney saw firsthand the problem that kept Southerners from turning to cotton as a cash crop.

The Cotton Gin

Cotton grew well across the South, with planters relying heavily on slave labor. But the cotton bolls that slaves

Harvesting crops on a New England farm in the 1830s. Children often helped with the work.

picked in the fields were littered with small, green sticky seeds, called staples. One slave might spend an entire day removing such seeds just to "clean" a single pound of cotton. Whitney invented a portable, tabletop contraption, which he called his "cotton engine" or "cotton gin" for short. It had dual rollers and simple rows of nails designed to pull cotton fibers through while leaving the seeds behind, and enabled a worker to clean cotton 300 times faster than by hand! Cotton would now pay, the South would become reli-

The Hartford Manufacturing Company cotton factory at Glastonbury, Connecticut, as depicted in a wood engraving of 1837. Early mills were mostly made of wood but from about 1820 they were made of brick.

ant on its cultivation, and any talk of slavery petering out by 1800 became foolish, indeed.

Expanded cotton cultivation only added fuel to the expansive economic fire. By 1820 cotton production had spread to Alabama, Mississippi, and Louisiana, and would soon reach Texas. But the economic boom did not last forever, of course, and by 1819 the American economy took a downturn. After years of war Europe had been able to return its battlefields to farm fields, and as a result the market for cotton and other American farm products fell across Europe. With this decline in cotton sales, cotton prices dropped, hitting a low of 10 cents a pound by 1823. With the decline in farm prices, public land sales plummeted and state banks and the Bank of the United States called in loans. This caused a short-lived depression, known as the Panic of 1819.

By the mid-1820s the economy was back on the rise, but some Americans emerged from those years of a poor economy blaming the Bank of the United States for their economic woes. The national bank had foreclosed on thousands of farmers, small operators, and others who could not pay their mortgages, all to protect, as their critics saw things, the selfish interests of their greedy stockholders. The Panic of 1819 had caused lower class Americans to see for the first time the power of big money—individuals who, they came to believe, were capable of controlling the national economic system to their own advantage. The result was that the Panic of 1819 helped set the stage for the next political era in American history—the Age of Jackson, otherwise known as the Age of the Common Man.

CANDIDATES JACKSON AND ADAMS

In 1824 Monroe was in the last year of his second term as president. He had been a popular chief executive, but the Panic of 1819 and the enactment of the Missouri Compromise, which limited the expansion of slavery in parts of the Louisiana Territory, had left his party—the Republicans—politically divided. Monroe knew the odds that another Virginian would follow him as president were slim, so he threw his support to his Secretary of State, Northerner John Quincy Adams. But the party nominated a state rights advocate from Georgia, William Crawford, Monroe's Secretary of the Treasury. Two further candidates threw their hats in the presidential ring: the Speaker of the House, Henry Clay, and Tennessee's favorite son, Andrew Jackson.

The 1824 election campaign revealed that the days of the "Era of Good Feelings" were long gone. The country's voters were divided, with Northerners supporting Adams (from Massachusetts), while Southerners rallied around Crawford. In the West, Clay was popular. But Andrew Jackson had supporters all over the country. When the election was held, Jackson won the popular vote, taking 153,000 to Adams's nearly 109,000. Clay and Crawford emerged almost neck and neck with 47,000 and 46,000 votes respectively. The electoral count was what mattered, however, and Jackson received 99 votes against Adams's 84, Crawford's 41, and Clay's 37. But Jackson did not walk away with the presidency.

Since Jackson's electoral votes equaled a plurality, not a majority, according to the Constitution the election decision had to be made by the House of Representatives. The House chooses from among the top three so Clay, being fourth, was out of the race, and Crawford soon experienced a debilitating stroke, knocking him out. This left only Jackson and Adams. With Clay no longer running, he had the power, as Speaker of the House, to influence the election. As he agreed on more political issues with Adams than with his fellow Westerner Jackson, Clay threw his support to the Massachusetts candidate. This ensured an Adams victory, giving him the presidency—the second Adams to hold the office.

Jackson and his supporters were furious, and even more so when President Adams appointed Clay as his Secretary of State. As noted by historian Allen Weinstein, men soon spoke of a "corrupt bargain" between the two politicians. Jackson had nothing good to say about Clay, claiming "The Judas of the West has closed the contract and will receive the thirty pieces of silver." Only a heavy snowfall kept Jackson's supporters from burning Adams in effigy during the inauguration in Washington City. Shortly after the election, Jackson's supporters set their sights on the 1828 election.

THE ELECTION OF 1828

Adams proved to be a capable, talented president, who enthusiastically embraced the nation's economic growth and westward movement. He was a brilliant individual, extremely well-read, articulate, and fluent in seven languages. (Each morning he read from the Bible in three of those languages—English, German, and French.) When he was young he had seen the world as a traveling companion to his father John Adams, during his father's various stints as a foreign diplomat. As president, Adams called for such innovations as a national university and national observatory, and for further explorations into the vast western interior of the United States. But many of his proposals were stymied or struck down by his political opponents, especially Senator Martin Van Buren of New York, who, according to historian Allen Weinstein, "worked to block every bill that the Adams administration put forth, regardless of its merit." By the last year of Adams's term as president, those same supporters of Andrew Jackson, the new party of Democrats, accused Adams of not having accomplished anything of any substance during his years in office.

The rematch campaign of 1828 brought President Adams and Andrew Jackson together again as opponents, and proved to be one of the bitterest campaigns in American history. It was also the first in which all nominations were made by state legislatures and during mass meetings called conventions, rather than by Congressional caucuses, an important political reform of the period. Ironically, when Jackson chose his vice presidential running mate, he picked John C. Calhoun, who was already serving as Adams's vice president!

Accusations flew back and forth between the supporters of each of the two candidates. Adams's men tried to cast a shadow on Jackson by distributing the "Coffin Handbill," which included a row of black coffins across the masthead. In the bill, Jackson was said to have ordered the executions of six Tennessee militiamen who had mutinied during the War of 1812. Jackson was also accused of stealing another man's wife. Jackson and Rachel Donelson Robards had married years earlier, after she thought her estranged husband had divorced her, but he had not actually done so. Mrs. Jackson, who was a devout and religious woman, was accused of being a bigamist, as she was married to two men at the same time. Even Jackson's mother was accused of being a prostitute whose clients had been British soldiers during the American Revolutionary War. Adams himself was accused of having provided an American prostitute for the Czar during his tenure as U.S. minister to Russia. (The "Coffin Handbill" accusation and Rachel being married to two men at the same time were true, but the other claims were false.)

Jackson emerged from the election the clear winner, however, sweeping the electoral count with 178 votes to Adams's 83. Jackson received 647,276 popular votes to 508,064 for Adams. The election had generated so much interest on the part of the American people that 800,000 more voted in 1828 than had voted in 1824! This was also due to voter qualifications having changed to eliminate or reduce the property qualification.

Between the election and Jackson's Inauguration, Rachel Jackson died of a heart attack on December 22, 1828. Her death grieved her 62-year-old husband, and Jackson blamed those who had leveled vicious accusations at her during the campaign. There was so much bad blood between Adams and Jackson that the president did not remain in Washington City for the inauguration, but left town to avoid any contact with the cantankerous, old Indian Fighter whose supporters referred to him affectionately as "Old Hickory."

4

The Age of Jackson

The people of the United States had never elected anyone like Andrew Jackson. He would be the last veteran of the Revolutionary War to be elected president. He was not part of the "Virginia Dynasty" that had dominated the presidency with the likes of Washington, Jefferson, Madison, and Monroe. And the country had never seen an inauguration as boisterous and wild as the one held in March 1829. Thousands of frontier families, backwoodsmen, yeoman farmers, and simple country people flocked to Washington to see their candidate take the presidency.

After Jackson took the Oath of Office, a grand reception was held at the Executive Mansion. People swarmed to the president's new home, where they grabbed cakes, ice cream, and orange punch. They stood on chairs in muddy boots, pulled down curtains, broke dishes, and pressed in so close to greet President Jackson that, according to historian Robert Remini, a Washington newspaper wrote how "The President, after having been literally nearly pressed to death & almost suffocated & torn to pieces by the people in their eagerness to shake hands with Old Hickory, had retreated through the back way or south front & had escaped to his lodgings at Gadsby's." The nation's common man had gained a voice, and that voice wanted to see what its new president was like. As for Jackson, he was about to preside over a new era in American history.

TAKING THE OFFICE BY STORM

When Jackson took office, much of his public career was behind him. He had served in the Tennessee legislature, as the state's governor, as a member of the U.S. Senate, as Governor of Florida, and as general of the Tennessee state militia and the U.S. Army. He was 62 years old, and in poor health, from both a bullet wound he had received decades earlier, which caused him to often spit up blood and pus, and from the various medicines he took for his ailments, drugs that contained harmful ingredients, including poisonous mercury. But Jackson proved forceful as president, more so than any chief executive before him and for decades to follow.

He set out to reform government from the outset. But his idea of reform was to replace unelected government bureaucrats with his own supporters, through a process soon called the "spoils system." Jackson called such replacements "rotation in office." In all, he dismissed 2,000 of 11,000 federal employees, about the same proportion of replacements that President Jefferson had made a generation earlier. But Jefferson had removed fewer officials for just "political" reasons.

INDIAN REMOVAL

Although Jackson was known prior to his presidency as an Indian fighter, his administration did not encourage direct warfare with Native Americans. Instead, a new and decisive phase in the historical clash between American Indians and white settlement was already underway. Despite his years of fighting Indians, Jackson had some sympathy for them and held the view that many other Americans did: Anglo-American expansion into the lands west of the Appalachian Mountains was threatening the survival of many of the eastern nations of native Americans; to survive, they needed to remove themselves from the path of white expansion.

In 1830 Congress passed the Indian Removal Act, which earmarked funds for negotiating with the various tribes in the East and relocating them onto portions of the Great Plains. To many non-Indians, this strategy seemed reasonable. It would allow Indians to maintain their worlds and their various cultures. They would be placed so far west—in modern-day Nebraska, Kansas, and Oklahoma—that they would be outside the course of white settlement and would be able to live at peace and in security.

The Seminole War Ends
Between 1830 and 1838 nearly all the Five Civilized Tribes (the Choctaw, Chickasaw, Creek, Cherokee, and Seminole) were expelled from their homes in the southern region of the United States to the designated Indian Territory, west of the Mississippi River. The Choctaw were among the first to go, starting in 1830, followed by the Creek in 1836, and the Chickasaw in 1837. In the northwest region, tribes including the Sac, Fox, Shawnee, Winnebago, and Pottawatomie were also moved into the West.

While some tribes cooperated, others, such as the Seminole in Georgia and Florida, did not. Led by a chieftain named Osceola, the Seminole balked and even went to war with the federal government in 1835 to defend their native lands. Some runaway black slaves joined in support of the Seminole. The Seminole War continued on for several years.

Jackson, who had fought the Seminole back in 1817–1818, sent U.S. forces to Florida, but the Seminole proved to be expert guerrilla fighters who attacked, then melted into local swamps. Osceola himself was captured in October 1837 and died the following year in an army fort. But the war dragged on until 1842, when the federal government abandoned its military efforts against the Indians. Many Seminoles had been killed by then and others had finally agreed to move west. But not all moved, and descendents of the Seminole may still be found in Florida today.

The Cherokee Are Forced West

While some Cherokee agreed to go west, others fought the government, but not in the usual way. They chose to fight by using the law. Many of the Cherokee had adopted "white" ways of life. They had assimilated, abandoning many of their traditional Indian cultural ways and choosing to wear "white" clothes, own wagons, build houses and log cabins, and even convert to Christianity. They lived in towns, had a written language, lived under a Cherokee Constitution, ran blacksmith shops and general stores, and supported schools. Since they lived "like whites," the Cherokee tried to stop the U.S. government from forcing them west by taking their case to court.

Two cases found their way to the U.S. Supreme Court. State officials in Georgia had tried to remove the Cherokee from their traditional lands when gold was discovered there, causing whites to encroach on those Indian lands. In *Cherokee Nation v. Georgia* (1831) and *Worcester v. Georgia* (1832), the Supreme Court supported the claim that the state of Georgia had no authority to negotiate with tribal representatives. These cases also established the concept of Indians as "sovereign nations," even as they also established the Indians as wards of the federal government.

Despite the Supreme Court's decisions, President Jackson did not enforce either of them. In 1835, U.S. officials negotiated with a small faction of Cherokee and drew up a treaty that many members of the tribe did not accept. But Jackson ordered federal troops to round up the uncooperative Cherokee and drive them to the western Indian Territory, with General Winfield Scott in command. Approximately 1,000 Cherokee escaped to the hill country of North Carolina and

Artist Robert Lindneux depicted the removal of the Cherokee Indians to the West in his oil painting entitled *The Trail of Tears*. Wagons were pulled by oxen, mules, and horses. Most people walked, with only the sick and elderly riding in the wagons.

hid out. Much later, the federal government established a reservation in the Smoky Mountains that even survives today. Other Cherokee were taken at bayonet point to today's Oklahoma along the "Trail of Tears," a march that killed thousands, due to a lack of food and frigid winter temperatures.

By the end of the 1830s most major Indian nations who had lived east of the Mississippi had been removed to the West. In all, those tribes had surrendered some 100 million

NATIVE AMERICANS FORCED WEST

The U.S. government established a network of routes or trails from Indian homelands east of the Mississippi to Indian Territory in Oklahoma.

Ferryboats took the Indians across the Tennessee, Ohio, and Mississipi Rivers. The complete journey took several weeks or months.

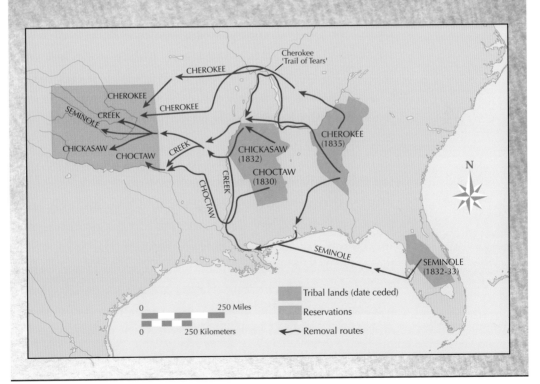

acres (40 million hectares) of land to the federal government. In return, they received about $68 million, along with 32 million acres (13 million ha.) of western land. They made new homes for themselves in a land that had little resemblance to the territories they had been forced to abandon, leaving shameful legacy on the part of the federal government.

THE TARIFF OF ABOMINATIONS

Earlier in 1828 Congress had passed a new tariff bill, which many Southerners did not support, calling it the "Tariff of Abominations." Generally, Southerners did not appreciate such tariffs, since they exported their agricultural products overseas in exchange for European manufactured goods and tariffs raised the cost of those manufactured items. Tariffs cost Southerners and hurt them economically. Vice President John C. Calhoun was among those who despised the new tariff. He anonymously wrote an opposition essay, called the *South Carolina Exposition and Protest,* in which he claimed that a state could legally nullify, or declare void, any federal law which the state determined had violated the Constitution, a view called the "doctrine of nullification." The courts had already claimed the power to make such decisions, however.

Jackson was furious when he learned Calhoun had written the nullification essay. Others in Congress were equally dismayed that the vice president could give his support to a political philosophy that could lead to the destruction of the Union. In 1830, a debate erupted on the Senate floor between Robert Hayne, from South Carolina, and Daniel Webster of Massachusetts. Hayne argued on behalf of nullification, stating that a state was sovereign in its own right and that the federal government could not force its support of any measure not to that state's liking. Webster reminded Hayne that it was the people, not the states, that made up the

Union and that all federal laws were binding on all American citizens alike. As historian David S. Reynolds notes, Webster made it clear that he wanted to see the country's leaders avoid secession at all costs, stating: "Liberty and Union, now and forever, one and inseparable!"

Jackson Gets Tough

Calhoun's doctrine of nullification was put to the test in 1832, when Congress passed a new tariff that raised custom duties, and Jackson signed the legislation. On November 24, 1832, South Carolina congressmen met in convention and adopted a resolution declaring the tariffs of 1828 and 1832 as "null and void." The convention of angry South Carolina officials vowed to secede from the Union if the federal government forced the payment of the new tariff rates. Calhoun supported the nullifiers and even resigned from the vice presidency on December 28, 1832, making him the first vice president to do so. However, Jackson had already been reelected in November and had dumped Calhoun as his vice president, picking up New Yorker Martin Van Buren as his new second. Calhoun was therefore a lame duck and had little to lose by resigning.

But Jackson responded with force. He threatened to send a warship and revenue vessels to Charleston Harbor, and he prepared to lead an army himself to force South Carolina back in line. With his brash style, he threatened to hang Calhoun if he caught him. Tension mounted until Henry Clay worked up a solution to the impasse. He hammered out an agreement, a compromise that provided tariff schedules to be lowered gradually over a period of nine years until 1842, when no duty would be set higher than 20 percent. (Parts of the "Tariff of Abominations" had set tariff rates at 50 percent!) On March 1, 1833, Congress passed the Compromise Tariff, along with a force bill, to nudge South Carolina into compliance by threatening military action, and Jackson signed both bills. South Carolinians accepted the compromise within two weeks, and a true crisis was averted.

THE BANK WAR

One of Jackson's main objectives during his presidency was to take on a foe he had opposed for many years—the Bank of the United States. Jackson had always thought the Bank to be unconstitutional. However, that issue had already been decided by an earlier Supreme Court decision, *McCulloch v. Maryland,* in which the Court had upheld the Bank's constitutionality. Despite the Court's decision, notes historian Allen Weinstein, Jackson told Martin Van Buren: "The Bank is trying to kill me, but I will kill it."

Jackson did not think the Bank had ever managed to establish a "uniform and sound" currency for the country. He was a "hard money" supporter, who thought money should be silver and gold coins, not paper. Yet his claim against the Bank was largely unfounded. He also thought the Bank represented a monopoly, one that threatened democratic government. And the Panic of 1819 had confirmed his worst fears: that the Bank was the enemy of the common man, those Westerners and Southerners who had supported him as a presidential candidate. Jackson believed the Bank of the United States supported only the wealthy Easterners who wielded great influence over the nation's economy, and that it did the biding of such interests at the expense of regular Americans. Jackson stated in 1832, as noted by historian Robert Remini: "It is to be regretted that the rich and powerful too often bend the acts of government to their selfish purposes." The president felt the government had taken steps to make "the rich richer and the potent more powerful [while] the humble members of society—the farmers, the mechanics, and laborers—who have neither the time nor the means of securing like favors to themselves, have a right to complain of the injustice of their Government."

Jackson should not have had the opportunity to do much damage to the Bank during his years in office. The Second Bank of the United States had been rechartered in 1816, providing a 20-year run for the Bank, which was slated to run out in 1836, Jackson's last year as president. But Henry Clay gave Jackson his opening. In 1832, four years before the Bank's charter was scheduled to end, Clay placed its recharter before Congress. He wanted to entice Jackson to veto the Bank, so that he could use this against Jackson during the election that year. Jackson took the bait, vetoed the Bank recharter, and then went on to defeat Clay in the election.

Land Speculation Leads to a Crisis

With the Bank of the United States officially scheduled to die out in four years, Jackson took the opportunity to try and kill it off early. He decided to remove all the government's deposits from the Bank, and then he placed those monies in 23 state banks of his choosing, called "pet banks." Many of these were unregulated banks, sometimes known as "wildcat banks," with loose banking practices, including loaning excessive amounts of money to land speculators with hopes of high returns and profits.

Land speculation at that time was a booming market. In 1834 speculators sold 4 million acres (1.6 million hectares) of land. This amount shot up to 15 million acres (6 million ha.) in 1835, and then 20 million acres (8 million ha.) by 1836. But in 1837 the land speculation bubble burst. Wildcat banks had overspeculated and even printed paper money, as bank notes, to back up their loans. But by then, most banks across the country had only one gold dollar on deposit for every 12 paper dollars. America's money was slipping dramatically in value, and the house of cards soon collapsed.

Jackson tried to stave off the economic avalanche, but he only managed to make matters worse. In the summer of 1836 he issued his "Specie Circular," an executive order that required all government land agents to accept only hard currency—gold or silver—as payment for land sales. This sent shockwaves across the West, where land speculators had been selling millions of acres, taking paper money as payment. The "Specie Circular" nearly dried up the land market. With little hard currency in circulation, people could not buy land, sales plummeted, and the government lost one of its most important sources of income—the sale of public lands. It all fell apart quickly. Prices and interest rates rose. Between 1834 and 1837 prices in America increased by 28

AN AGE OF PRACTICAL INVENTIONS

Almost no factories had existed in America during the Colonial Period, but the end of the eighteenth century saw the beginnings of such infant industries. One of the earliest factories in America was constructed by an English immigrant, named Samuel Slater, who had built such work places in Great Britain before coming to the United States to do the same. In 1790 Slater's textile mill was opened in Rhode Island and during the next 20 years additional factory mills were constructed.

The early nineteenth century witnessed a trove of important inventions, each of which made its own unique contribution to American life. Steam power was harnessed and used to power mills, factories, steamboats, and early railroads. The first practical, commercially profitable steamboat was invented in 1807 by a New Yorker named Robert Fulton. Steam power was first used to develop early railroads in England. America's first railroad locomotive was built by Peter Cooper in 1830. Steam-powered travel provided faster transportation on land and on interior rivers and lakes than had ever been previously imagined.

percent! The money supply was inflated. Businesses were overextended. The Bank of the United States called in piles of loans, including those to states that had borrowed to pay for internal improvements, such as canals and railroads. The Bank of the United States and other Eastern banks refused to accept paper money for debt payments. State banks, having dramatically overextended themselves, were driven out of business. The Panic of 1837 loomed across the country.

An Economic Mess

Perhaps ironically, Jackson was not blamed for the economic collapse, even though it was partially of his making. Many factors, including bank collapses, did not kick in until the

Farmers found their work eased by such inventions as John Deere's steel plow (1837) and Cyrus McCormick's automatic reaping machine (1831), which replaced workers who had previously cut grain with hand-held scythes.

In 1844 an American inventor, Samuel F. B. Morse, developed a working model of the first magnetic telegraph. This invention provided instant communication over long distances, something never previously achieved in the history of humankind.

While the inventor of the cotton gin, Eli Whitney, had also pioneered the manufacturing system that relied on interchangeable parts in gun manufacture, it was Samuel Colt who made the first successful, repeating revolver (1836) using interchangeable parts.

Everything from the sewing machine (1846) to the rotary printing press (1847), suspension bridges spanning major rivers (1847), an efficient steel-making process (1852), the passenger elevator (1853), and the vacuum evaporator for canning food products with a long shelf life (1846) came into reality during the years prior to the Civil War. America became more reliant on such inventions for quicker transportation, better communication, and greater productivity.

spring of 1837, when Jackson was already out of office and a new president, former vice president Martin Van Buren, was the chief executive. The depression was widespread. In New York City alone, 50,000 people became unemployed.

A view of Utica, New York, in 1838. Starting around 1800, many farmers and their families moved to urban areas to find better lives. While cities developed quickly, towns remained rural for decades.

Despite some temporary recovery in 1838, the panic continued through 1843.

Van Buren was unable to cope with the economic mess.
With no Bank of the United States by 1837, he proposed
a new regional treasury system in an effort to take federal
monies out of the unstable state banks where Jackson had
put them. But his Independent Treasury Act, which passed
Congress in 1840, only allowed the newly established treasury branches to accept gold and silver coins (specie), not
paper money. These federal branch banks would not accept
checks drawn on state banks, which simply deprived such
banks of specie, making them even more unstable. It took
years before the American economic system was back on its
feet and thriving again. Jackson's economic policies, including his destruction of the Bank of the United States and his
limited view of money, had helped create a monster.

NEW AMERICAN POLITICS

Even though Jackson's economic policies only pushed the
United States into a serious depression, he remained a popular president throughout his eight years in office, a man of
the people. His supporters—the "common man"—included
frontiersmen, artisans, day laborers, and yeoman farmers
and many of them felt about the Bank of the United States as
Jackson did. It seemed at times that, no matter what Jackson
did, he remained the great symbol for the nation's middle
and underclasses. He was seen as a leader who stood up to
the powerful and wealthy.

Democrats and Whigs

Prior to Jackson's presidency, the old Democratic-Republican
Party had split into the National Republicans and the Demo-
crats. It was the Democrat wing of the party that provided
Jackson's political core. But this new party, the Democrats,

remained intact even after Jackson finished his presidency and retired back to Tennessee, becoming the most viable and long-lasting of the two parties. In fact from 1828 to 1860 the Democrats dominated American politics, winning the presidency in each election with only two exceptions—1840 and 1848.

As for the National Republicans, they did not even survive the Jackson presidency. But, from the rubble of the abandoned National Republicans, another party was formed. It was first little more than an anti-Jackson coalition, whose members saw Jackson as too powerful, too forceful. Some referred to Jackson as "King Andrew," with some political cartoons showing the president dressed in royal robes, a crown on his head, his fist clenching a scepter. With this "royal" image of Jackson, the new party soon took on the label of the Whigs—the name of a group of Patriots of 1775 who were opposed to autocratic rule. The Whigs sometimes proved a strong opposition force to Jackson. Party members first polled significant numbers in congressional elections in 1834, the midway point of Jackson's second term. By the 1840s, the Whigs were nearly equal in political power with the Democrats. In national elections, both parties polled similar numbers of votes. The Whigs took a lesson from Jackson's political legacy as president. They attempted to sell themselves as the party of the common voters, hoping to draw some of Jackson's supporters away from the Democrats.

More People Get the Vote

Both the Democrats and the Whigs took significant steps to change voting qualifications across the United States and allow more people to vote. Those people would still be white males, but the new qualifications included reducing or eliminating the property qualification for voting. The result of such changes meant that many more Americans were able to cast ballots than ever before. In 1824 approximately 360,000 voted. But just four years later the number of voters increased to 1.1 million. That number continued to rise until it reached 2.4 million voters in the 1840 election.

But the rise in the number of voters does not tell the full story. The proportion of eligible voters who cast ballots increased as well. In 1824 only around 27 percent of those eligible to vote actually did so. But through the elections from 1828 to 1836, the percentage of eligible voters who cast ballots rose to approximately 55 percent. By 1840 the percentage of involved voters had risen to a whopping 80 percent—four out of five eligible voters. All this means that the two political parties were popular with their own constituencies, were responsive to the political will of the people, and that barriers limiting the percentage of white males who cast their votes had been broken down. Unfortunately, however, women continued to be denied the privilege of voting.

There were differences between the two parties, to be certain. The Whigs supported a national bank, paper currency, and the expansion of business corporations. The Democrats did not generally endorse these issues. Whigs also favored the advancement of social and humanitarian reforms in America, such as the development of a public school system, a temperance movement to limit alcohol consumption, prison and asylum reforms, and the abolition of capital punishment. Again, Democrats were typically lukewarm on these issues.

While the American political system was rapidly changing to accommodate the "common man," President Martin Van Buren quickly proved to be less popular than Andrew Jackson. He struggled through his term of office with a sliding economy. He was elected in 1836 against three Whig challengers—William Henry Harrison, Daniel Webster, and

Hugh Lawson White—each chosen to appeal to a given region of the country. The Whigs had hoped to split the vote as dramatically as had happened in 1824 and throw the election into the House of Representatives, but the move failed, with Van Buren winning nearly 51 percent of the vote to 49 percent for his three opponents combined.

THE ELECTION OF 1840

However, with the poor economy during the Van Buren presidency, the Whigs felt confident in 1840 that they had a sure shot at gaining the leadership of the executive branch. Again they chose William Henry Harrison. Like Jackson, he was an aging Indian fighter, a former Western governor (of Indiana), and a well-known national figure. The party selected John Tyler, a Virginia senator, as his running mate. Tyler, a former Democrat, had left that party over Jackson's destruction of the Bank of the United States.

The 1840 election proved as rousing as any to date. There were songs and slogans in support of each party's candidate. Whigs chanted at rallies and other public gatherings, "Van, Van, Van; Oh! Van is a used-up man!" Tennessee Congressman Davy Crockett even claimed that Van Buren wore silk stockings and a corset. Democrats formed political groups called O.K. Clubs. Van Buren, from an old Dutch family, was raised in the New York settlement of Old Kinderhook. In their slogans, Van Buren was referred to as "O.K." This became the likely origin of the common term used today to indicate that something is acceptable. Perhaps the best remembered slogan was in support of Harrison, who in 1811 had led military forces against the Shawnee in the battle of Tippecanoe. The slogan—"Tippecanoe and Tyler, Too"—reminded the voters of their candidate's past as an Indian fighter.

Neither candidate actively campaigned in 1840, as it was not the custom for candidates to do so in that era. But the campaign was filled with political rallies and parades, bon-fires and fish fries, all designed to appeal to the "common man." When Democrats accused Harrison of being little more than a tooth-sucking rube who lived in a log cabin on the frontier, where he drank hard cider, the Whigs turned it into a positive, running their man as the "log cabin and hard cider" candidate. In the end, this image appealed to voters, who turned out in record numbers. With a voter turnout of 80 percent, Harrison was elected with 1.27 million votes, to Van Buren's 1.12 million votes. As president, Harrison intended to support such Whig measures as a new national bank and higher tariffs, but he did not live to do so. Within a month of his inauguration in March 1841, the 68-year-old Harrison died of pneumonia, making him the first president to die in office.

5

A New American Spirit

As Americans entered the nineteenth century, many did so with enthusiasm and great anticipation concerning the young republic's future. In newspapers, sermons, and speeches, the nation's leaders called for the people of the United States to take hold of the opportunities before them. The spirit of the new century, of a new age, was, as noted by historian Robert Remini: "Go ahead. Go ahead... Go ahead is the order of the day, the real motto of the country." Massachusetts Senator Daniel Webster, known for his oratory, suggested that "Our age is full of excitement," and he was, perhaps, telling the truth more than he knew.

During the first 50 years of the nineteenth century Americans experienced the most rapid period of change in their country's history to date. There were new inventions, new means of travel and communication, and new lands to be conquered in the West. Immigrants from Europe were streaming to America by the thousands, seeking new opportunities.

The American people were intent on building two worlds for themselves. The first was materialistic, founded on business, trade, commerce, and the personal accumulation of wealth. As the European visitor Alexis de Tocqueville wrote in his book, *Democracy in America*: "No man in America is contented to be poor or expects to continue so." The second world was more philosophical, even spiritual. Many excited

A view of West Point on the Hudson River with Robert Fulton's steamboat *Clermont* steaming upstream from New York to Albany. Fulton pioneered long-distance journeys along many of America's longest rivers.

Americans became convinced that they lived in the greatest nation in the world. They believed that humans could be made nearly perfect by working hard to improve their society, especially by working on behalf of those who were downtrodden, oppressed, and less fortunate. Reform became the order of the day. In short, if America had problems, Americans should work to fix them, to improve their society. Many were motivated to participate in the reform movements of the era through their religion. They were drawn by their faith, and they set themselves to providing improvements in their world.

A REAWAKENED AMERICA

As the United States entered the nineteenth century, a great wave of religious change swept across the country, led by various Protestant faith traditions. An earlier movement had occurred between 1740 and 1760, called the Great Awakening. This new religious revival period was therefore known as the Second Great Awakening. While the theologian Jonathan Edwards had led the first revival period, one of his students, Nathaniel Taylor, would take the forefront of this latest spiritual movement. (One of Taylor's theology professors at Yale, Timothy Dwight, was a grandson of Edwards.)

Just as Edwards and Dwight had emphasized the need for a personal relationship between an individual Christian and God, so did Taylor. But he took the concept of salvation even further. An earlier theology, Calvinism, had taught that souls were predestined for either eternal reward or punishment, but Taylor believed that salvation was available to all who might seek it. He placed greater emphasis on an individual's "free will."

Other ministers taught the same message and were soon out preaching their new gospel in large "revival meetings." Such meetings became commonplace across the country, but were perhaps most effective in frontier regions, where life was dangerous and difficult and salvation could well be the only hope of a better life. A meeting might begin on a Thursday and continue until the following Tuesday. As many as 25,000 people might attend to hear sermons delivered by up to 40 preachers, sometimes several at once, each taking a corner of an open field or meadow. These preachers delivered fiery sermons, sometimes describing the threat of hell. At such night meetings, with flaming torches casting eerie shadows, people often could not help but respond emotionally, some in fear, some on a spiritual high. It was common at such revivals for people to weep and wail loudly, and even convulse with jerking spasms, leap about, or roll on the ground.

This revival movement sometimes led to splits in such old line Protestant groups as the Presbyterians, Baptists, and Methodists. Whole new Christian sects emerged, such as the Church of Jesus Christ of Latter-Day Saints (the Mormons) and the Seventh-Day Adventists. There were the Campbellites, Christians who believed that religious conversion was an individual matter, that the Bible represented the only true source of God's testament to the world, and that baptism, considered essential for salvation, was only for adults, and should take the form of whole body immersion. These followers of the Scottish theologian and minister, Alexander Campbell, eventually became known as the Disciples of Christ. Today, members of the Christian Church and the Churches of Christ, largely scattered across the southern states, are the inheritors of the Campbellite faith.

"HEAVEN ON EARTH"

During the early decades of the nineteenth century, some Americans came to believe in the possibility of an ideal or Utopian community, where members could live in harmony with one another. Such groups and organizations had lofty goals, hoping to create closed, engineered, nearly perfect communities in which labor was pooled, resources shared, and the injustices and failures of American society were eliminated. Historian Michael Barkun quotes one utopian member in 1844 summing up the purpose of these socio-economic systems: "Our ulterior aim [was] nothing less than Heaven on Earth." Often, such groups were not just interested in social reform, but were religious in nature, too.

The Shakers

One group that combined religious utopianism and social reform was the Shakers. Founded in the late eighteenth century by English immigrant Mother Ann Lee, the Shakers were a religious commune whose members thought the end of the world was coming soon. For that reason, they preached a total rejection of sin. Ann Lee also taught that God had both female and male characteristics and that all sexual activity was evil. Thus, Shakers were expected to be celibate.

While Shakers did not participate in sexual activity, they did practice highly emotional dancing, including shaking. This was an important activity, since the Shakers believed they should express emotion in their religion. Shakers allowed both men and women to be elders and deacons. The members lived together, shared everything, and emphasized quiet, simple living, in an ordered world free from sin. These elements were mirrored in the Shakers' building designs and furniture making.

The element of simplicity among the Shakers was put into verse by a Shaker composer, Joseph Brackett, in 1848 and sung during some versions of Shaker dance. The song *Simple Gifts* refers to the Shaker notion of a "gift"—a God-given talent or unique insight held by each Shaker member. One version of the song included the lines:

'Tis the gift to be simple, 'tis the gift to be free,
'Tis the gift to come down where we ought to be;
And when we find ourselves in the place just right,
'Twill be in the valley of love and delight.
When true simplicity is gain'd,
To bow and to bend we shan't be asham'd
To turn, turn, will be our delight,
Till by turning, turning we come round right.

In the twentieth century, this song was adapted by the American composer Aaron Copland for his *Appalachian Spring* suite. By 1826 there were 18 Shaker communities scattered across eight states, but even by 1860 membership stood at only 6,000.

Shaker men and women dancing in their traditional fashion at a religious meeting around 1840.

The Rappites and the Amana Colonies

There were several German utopian groups, established by immigrants from the Old Country. One such group, the Rappites, was founded in 1804 by George Rapp, who brought over 600 separatists from the Lutheran Church. They settled along the banks of Indiana's Wabash River, where they built a colony called Harmony. The Rappites believed Jesus' second coming was going to be very soon. They did not engage in sexual activities; they farmed and shared everything with each other; and they enjoyed the music of their German immigrant band. Rapp established another commune called Economy in Pennnsylvania before he died in 1847. The last member of his community died toward the end of the nineteenth century.

Another German group was the Amana Society, or the Community of the True Inspiration. This society was not based on following a charismatic leader, but was a group of 700 people who were drawn together after immigrating to America from the German state of Hesse. After some colonizing in New York, they moved out to southeastern Iowa, where they established seven villages known as the Amana Colonies. They took the name "Amana" from the Old Testament's *Song of Solomon*. Unlike the Shakers and Rappites, they were not a celibate group. The Amanans continued to live communally until 1932, and even today still practice their old religion. The Amana Colonies are best known to the outside world for the manufacture of appliances, such as refrigerators, stoves, and microwaves.

EXPERIMENTS IN SOCIALISM

Other utopian communities were established in America between the 1820s and 1840s, many based on a concept of brotherhood, cooperation, and often, socialism. There were the Associationists, established by Albert Brisbane during the 1840s, who worked out a mathematical equation of socialism. By following the ideas of the French social theorist Charles Fourier, Brisbane had become convinced that capitalism was an inefficient system, one that doled out more advantages to some and fewer to others. He planned rigid communities he called "phalanxes," each having a membership of exactly 1,620 people, among whom each of the needed job skills would be represented. They would live on 6,000 acres (2,400 hectares) of land and create a self-sustaining economic and social world. Even the children were a resource, to be used as trash collectors, since they liked to play outside in the dirt.

Brisbane sold his experiment as a model of Christian communism, in which each believer would share with his neighbor. Although his plan was based on socialism, he did not ban private property, but each member owned shares in his phalanx. In total, 28 phalanxes were established, most in the North, but a couple were based in Louisiana. These experiments in retooling the socio-economic order did not last long—none more than a dozen or so years. One problem that continually plagued these unique communistic states was that they never created a sense of common identity among their residents. People came and went with regularity and the system was never completely closed off from the outside world. Established during the years of economic depression in America, many members did not stay when the overall economy improved.

New Harmony

In 1824 George Rapp sold the land of his colony Harmony to another utopian innovator, Scottish-immigrant industrialist Robert Owen. Owen quickly set about establishing his own utopian experiment—simply named New Harmony. Owen had seen the abuses of industrialization firsthand back in

Britain and had come to the conclusion that the key to eliminating poverty among the working class was to place workers in self-operating, self-sustaining communes. His intentions to retool American society through his social experiment are noted by historian Mark Holloway, who quotes Owen as stating:

> I am come to this country to introduce an entire new system of society; to change it from an ignorant, selfish system to an enlightened social system which shall gradually unite all interests into one and remove all causes for contest between individuals.

Because it was his background, Owen's commune was based around a textile mill built on the commune's property along the Wabash River. New Harmony became a radical place. The workers made their own decisions about how the commune should be run and soon established an eight-hour working day, when most Americans labored daily between 12 and 16 hours, maybe more. They also operated a communal school for both boys and girls.

Perhaps somewhat unique to Owen's concept of a utopian society was the elimination of all religion. He did not allow the practice of any faith tradition in New Harmony. Equally radical were his views in support of women's rights and birth control. Members could live as married couples, although Owen did not support the institution himself, but it was expected that the commune would raise the children. As a result, children did not live with their parents.

Owen's experiment lasted just two years, then collapsed. The factory failed and closed down in 1827, and Owen's converts drifted apart and moved elsewhere. But during the three or four decades that followed, at least 18 other utopian communities were established in the United States that used

Owen's utopian model as their own, even though they had no ties to the Scottish socialist. And it was Owen's followers in Britain who actually coined the term "socialist."

The Oneida Community

One later utopian group was the Oneida Community established in central New York by John Humphrey Noyes. This group promoted a strange combination of religious beliefs and sexual freedoms. In earlier years Noyes had been a student at Andover Theological Seminary and Yale, where he developed odd religious ideas—so odd that no church would ordain him as a minister. He believed that the second coming of Jesus Christ had already taken place, back in 70 C.E., at the time the Jewish temple in Jerusalem was destroyed by the Romans, and that Jesus had left instructions for establishing a new Christian kingdom on earth. That new kingdom would only become reality when, according to Noyes, a small group of committed Christians created a new society, one perfected by being based on communal living and radical approaches to previously accepted social systems.

After studying other utopian groups, including the Owenites and the Shakers, Noyes established a small commune of followers in Putney, Vermont. He wrote a book, *Bible Communism* (1848), as the guide for his new social order. His colony of "Perfectionists" shared everything in common. Those who joined even shared one another in an open system of relationships, known as complex marriage, in which all the men were "married" to all the women. When Vermont officials heard of this arrangement, they accused Noyes of perpetuating adultery. He and his group of 31 adults and 14 children fled to New York, where they built another commune near the town of Oneida. There, they lived without outside interference for many years and grew to a group of more than 200.

The commune supported itself by making and selling animal traps. The women of the Oneida community were among the most liberated of the time, taking to cutting their hair short and wearing pants called "bloomer garments" under their skirts, which gave them greater freedom of movement. Historian Daniel Walker Howe notes one Oneida woman who professed: "We believed we were living under a system which the whole world would sooner or later adopt."

But the colony did not last more than a couple of generations. By 1880, John Noyes decided that his complex mar-

THE MORMONS

Some utopian societies and new religious groups experienced problems in being accepted by those on the outside—regular Americans who lived in mainstream society. Sometimes a new religious sect or strange utopian group might be hounded, or even persecuted, by local residents. One group who faced antagonism from their American neighbors chose a unique means of escape: They decided to leave the United States completely and move into the great untamed expanse of the West.

The Church of Jesus Christ of Latter-Day Saints was founded in 1827 by a New Yorker named Joseph Smith, who claimed he had been visited by an angel named Moroni, son of the prophet Mormon. The angel allegedly provided Smith with a new revelation, which became the *Book of Mormon*.

Smith used the *Book of Mormon* as the basis for a new Christian religion, one he claimed represented the true church. As a religious movement, the Mormons separated themselves from everyone else— those they called Gentiles—and became known for their closed social structure and mysterious religious customs and ideas. Rumors eventually circulated that Mormon men were engaging in polygamy, the practice of marrying multiple women. By this time, the Mormons had been

riage system had not worked, and the whole communistic social system was ended. In fact, Noyes formed the Oneida Community, Ltd. and sold stock in the new company, which became famous for its fine silverware.

THE TRANSCENDENTALISTS

While early nineteenth century America witnessed the establishment of many unique groups of utopians and communal systems, the vast majority of Americans remained attached to American society and to the standard Christian groups.

driven out of New York to Ohio, and then forced out to Missouri, where the state's governor threatened to have the group exterminated. Smith then moved his Saints to Illinois, where in 1839 they established a settlement they called Nauvoo. Here, the sect flourished for several years.

When the rumors of polygamy turned out to be true, Smith and his Saints were again targeted by locals. Violence erupted, and Joseph Smith and his brother were killed by a mob in Carthage, Illinois. The new Mormon leader, a tall Vermont carpenter named Brigham Young, decided his Saints could no longer live among their Gentile neighbors. He studied maps drawn by western explorers and decided he would move his church members out west to

the Valley of the Great Salt Lake, then in Spanish territory. All the Nauvoo community turned to wagon making, even building them in their temple.

In 1846, a pioneering group of Mormons left for the West with Brigham Young leading them. After a difficult winter spent in Iowa along the banks of the Missouri River, a party of 73 wagons left for the Salt Lake Valley in the spring of 1847. They followed the Oregon Trail and reached Fort Bridger by mid-June. Young then directed his party of religious followers south off the main trail and they soon reached the lake. Here, the Mormons established a great community, which soon included thousands of their brethren. This unique sect had finally found a home.

Within some of those groups, however, significant changes took place. The Puritans had helped establish several early British colonies in the 1600s. Later generations of Puritans developed into the Congregationalists of the eighteenth century. They continued to hold to the Reformation theology of John Calvin, who had preached predestination and the total sinfulness of human beings. Calvinism had also taught that infants were not born innocent, but were born under the sin that had been brought into the world according to the Biblical story of Adam and Eve.

Unitarianism

Now a new generation of Congregationalists broke off from the main sect and established a new group, called the Unitarians. It appealed to the better-educated, more affluent descendants of New England Puritans. Unitarians did not believe in the Trinity; they believed in a single God. Jesus was not the son of God: He was just an exemplary teacher. They also denied that babies were conceived in sin or that humans were born totally depraved. Unitarians were hopeful people who believed men and women were, by nature, good; that God was not a vengeful, punishing Being, but a kind and loving Father. Among their most important ministers of the early nineteenth century was William Ellery Channing, minister of the Federal Street Church in Boston. He taught that humans should follow their consciences, which would instinctively lead to good works, and that a primary goal of believers was to carry out humanitarian reform.

In time, some followers found Unitarianism to be insufficient for them. By the 1830s, a small group of intellectuals living close to one another at Concord, outside Boston, began meeting in the home of the Unitarian minister, Ralph Waldo Emerson. They spent their times together discussing their religious ideals and eventually called themselves the Transcendental Club. The group included several of Emerson's Concord neighbors, such as Henry David Thoreau, Nathaniel Hawthorne, Bronson Alcott, and his daughter, Louisa May Alcott—all destined to find their place in the pages of American literature.

Brook Farm

The Transcendental Club was not exactly a church, but it did discuss theology. Followers rejected John Calvin's teaching and held to the ideal that man was essentially good and that God equated love. They believed that an element of God lived in everyone and that human nature was not only good, but even held an element of divinity. Their idealistic faith led the Transcendentalists to trust that humans had an internal "intuition," a natural-born knowledge of what is right and just. Some members of the group established a community called Brook Farm in West Roxbury, Massachusetts, but the group did not last long. When a fire destroyed several of their buildings in 1846, the group went bankrupt and never recovered.

While the Transcendentalists were never large in number and always had a limited appeal, due to the high level of intellectualism among its members, the group was one of those that preached the value of reform in early nineteenth century America. The Transcendentalists saw materialism all around them with many people seeking after money and personal gain. Society was corrupt, the Transcendentalists were certain, and it needed to be uncorrupted and improved. Historian Robert Remini notes Emerson's perspective:

"What is man born for but to be a Reformer, a Re-Maker of what man has made, a renouncer of lies, a restorer of truth and good, imitating that great Nature which embosoms us all?"

He saw a future America, where reform had swept away the vices and problems of society, one in which do-gooding men and women lived "to raise the life of man by putting it in harmony with his idea of the Beautiful and the Just."

AN ERA OF REFORM

The call for reform in the United States was trumpeted, not only by the Transcendentalists, but by mainline Christian churches—Protestant and Catholic alike—as well as by many of the unique communal groups. The reformers of the 1820s, 1830s, 1840s, and even beyond focused on a wide variety of perceived social ills, seeking to change the destructive nature of American society and bring about an improved world. As one of the most popular Protestant evangelical ministers of early nineteenth century America said, his words noted by historian Robert Remini, "The evils have been exhibited, the call has been made for reform… Away with the idea that Christians can remain neutral and keep still, and yet enjoy the approbation [approval] and blessing of God."

Reformers came out of the woodwork, set and ready to retool American social systems. They called for improvements in prisons, such as individual cells, where criminals could be separated from one another, thus cutting down on the potential for one to further corrupt another. In a cell, the convict could reconsider his or her life, seek forgiveness and become a penitent person, thus a new name for American prisons—penitentiaries.

Some reformers advocated an end to prostitution in the United States, which was legal in many parts of the country during the early nineteenth century. Female Moral Reform Societies led a crusade against prostitution, often not to condemn the prostitute, but to assist such women in finding better jobs and other opportunities. Dorothea Dix, a Boston school teacher, championed the rights of the mentally ill by petitioning the Massachusetts legislature to build humane asylums. She carried on her campaign for nearly 50 years.

There were assistance programs for housing and farms for those living under grinding poverty and advocates for better working conditions for America's laborers. A widespread temperance movement included 5,000 state and local temperance societies, claiming a total of a million members. Between 1800 and 1830 the annual per capita consumption of alcohol had risen from 3 gallons to more than 7 gallons (14 to 32 liters). Through the temperance movement, by the mid-1840s the rate had fallen to just below two gallons (9 L). Some states, such as Maine, banned the sale of alcohol completely—except for medicinal purposes.

Women's Rights

A significant women's rights movement also took root. In 1848 the first Women's Rights Convention was held at Seneca Falls, New York, where 300 delegates (including some 40 men) adopted a statement paraphrasing the *Declaration of Independence*, that "all men and women are created equal." The document, *The Declaration of Sentiments and Resolutions*, listed several demands, including an end to such legal traditions as preventing married women from signing contracts and fathers automatically receiving the children in a case of divorce, while calling for greater educational opportunities. Historian Siegerman notes the words of one female attendee at the conference: "Most women accepted [their] condition of society as normal and God-ordained. . . But every fibre of my being rebelled."

The women's rights movement was led by such women as Lucretia Mott, Susan B. Anthony, and Elizabeth Cady Stanton. During the decades prior to the Civil War, the movement managed several victories, persuading a few states to give married women control over their own property and to open public schools to girls. Those public schools were the result of another reform movement, one led by Horace Mann, who, during the 1840s as Secretary of the Massachusetts Board of Education, called for more state support of education. He encouraged compulsory attendance laws and free public schools across the country. Just before his death, Mann spoke to the graduating class of Antioch College in Ohio. Historian Remini notes Mann's words: "Be ashamed to die until you have won some victory for humanity."

Opposition to Slavery

Perhaps one of the most important reform movements of the era was the abolitionist movement—those who were opposed to the institution of slavery. While slavery had always been a part of life in colonial America and later in the young republic, the holding of black slaves had become absolutely hated by those who had come to believe that good, Christian people cannot, of conscience, own another human being for the purpose of profiting from his or her forced labor. By 1804, slavery had been abolished in every northern state, but it was still prevalent elsewhere. By the 1830s, the American abolitionist movement had planted significant roots, to an extent due to the efforts of reformers such as William Lloyd Garrison. While the vast majority of Americans during the three decades leading up to the Civil War considered the abolitionists to be little more than wild-eyed fanatics, eventually their cause won over, helping to bring about an end to slavery in America by 1865. By then, of course, the nation had experienced the devastation of the Civil War, a conflict brought on by the recurring struggle over slavery and its expansion.

6

The Reach of the American Empire

Following the American purchase of Louisiana in 1803, the vast lands of the West, stretching from the Mississippi River to the Pacific Coast, were in the hands of three different world powers: the United States, Spain, and Great Britain. Spain claimed the lands of the Southwest, from the region they called the Californios to the northern province of Tejas. The British claimed the Oregon Country, which included today's states of Washington, Oregon, and Idaho. The Americans held the remainder, which was Louisiana. No one knew at the outset of the 1800s which power would dominate the West, or whether these various powers would each control their corner of the lands that included the Great Plains, the Rocky Mountains, and the Pacific Coast. In addition, there were scores of Indian nations living in every remote corner of this great expanse of territory, peoples who had called these places their homes for hundreds of years. The answer to the question of who would domi-

nate the West came during the early decades of the nineteenth century. It would be the Americans.

Statehood had moved further west than ever during the
age of Jackson. Arkansas entered the Union in 1836 and
Michigan in 1837, followed by a spate of new entries: Florida and Texas (1845), Iowa (1846), and Wisconsin (1848).
Fueling the country's drive to claim the West as its own
was a geographic philosophy based on American republi-
canism. In 1845 that philosophy received a name, when a
Democratic magazine editor, John L. O'Sullivan, writing in
the *United States Magazine and Democratic Review*, suggested
that God favored the spread of democracy and capitalism
across the West to the Pacific. Notes historian Allen Weinstein, O'Sullivan claimed Americans had a "manifest destiny
to overspread the continent allotted by Providence for the
free development of our yearly multiplying millions." The
expression "manifest destiny" became the siren call inspir-
ing Americans to go West. (At that time the word "manifest"
was synonymous with "obvious".)

THE TEXAS REVOLUTION

The nineteenth century witnessed a great increase in the
number of Americans pushing west of the Mississippi River.
During the 1820s, 1830s, and 1840s portions of the West
were in the hands of foreign powers—including Mexico, the
British, even the Russians—so the movement of Americans
ever westward represented a threat. Mexico, especially, felt
the challenge of this great American swell across the Great
Plains.

The Mexicans, who had overthrown their Spanish colo-
nizers in 1821, sought to control the movement of Americans into their northern province of Tejas. During the early
1820s the new Mexican government offered limited land
grants, which encouraged Stephen Austin, a Missourian, to

organize the first American colony in Tejas. Thousands of U.S. citizens poured into the vast borderlands and soon more than 20 American "colonies" existed. A decade after Austin's group had been established, General Antonio Lopez de Santa Anna was elected as president of Mexico. Though many settlers in Texas hoped that Santa Anna's election would mean greater representation for Texans in the Mexican government, it soon became apparent that Santa Anna intended to limit the freedom of Americans with more restrictions and less self-government.

After petitioning the Mexican government in vain for a lessening of controls, the Texans rebelled, and on March 2, 1836, declared their independence. President Jackson watched events from Washington, but did not campaign on behalf of Texas independence, staying decidedly neutral as he actually hoped to buy Texas from Mexico. The Texas Revolution soon witnessed the appointment of Sam Houston, a leading Texas citizen, as commander-in-chief of the Texans' army. Houston was a former member of the U.S. House of Representatives and former governor, who had left his native Tennessee after scandals involving his heavy drinking (the Osage Indians called him "Big Drunk") and his estrangement from his wife. A protégé of Andrew Jackson, he was a friend of the Cherokee. He had lived with them for a time and had even represented them in Washington on two occasions, where he exposed fraud against them on the part of the federal government.

The Battle of the Alamo

Santa Anna responded by taking 6,000 Mexican troops north to San Antonio, the provincial capital of Texas, where he attacked a garrison of 187 Texans at a mission-fortress called the Alamo. This small band of Texans, which included several Mexican *Tejanos,* held off thousands of Santa Anna's

The storming of the Alamo at San Antonio, Texas, by General Santa Anna and his troops on March 6, 1836. To the Texans, the battle was one of liberty. On defeat, they declared, "Remember the Alamo."

soldiers for 13 days until, on March 6, 1836, the Mexicans finally breached the walls and annihilated the entire garrison. Among those present inside the Alamo were the famed Tennessee backwoodsman, Davy Crockett, and Jim Bowie, who carried a type of large knife that was later named after him. Two weeks later and 60 miles (100 kilometers) down the San Antonio River from the Alamo, Santa Anna's army overran another group of Texans at Goliad, where the Mexicans executed 430 men.

As noted by historian Richard Kluger, following the massacres at the Alamo and at Goliad, Houston stated in anger: "The day of just retribution ought not to be deferred." Seeking revenge and eager to bolster their call for independence, Sam Houston and his Texas force led a surprise attack on Santa Anna's army at the battle of San Jacinto on April 21, 1836. Houston's men, in an attack that took less than half an hour, killed nearly half of the Mexican force (630 men) and captured the remainder, including Santa Anna himself. Only two Texans were killed and 20 or so wounded, including Houston, who had taken a musket ball in his right tibia above the knee. On May 14 the Mexican general signed the Treaty of Velasco, which ended the revolution by recognizing Texas as an independent republic. Santa Anna agreed to the Rio Grande as the border between Mexico and Texas, although he repudiated the treaty once he was set free and had returned to Mexico City. Houston, the hero of the revolution, was elected as the first president of the new Republic of Texas. For nearly ten years, Texas was its own nation.

THE OREGON COUNTRY

While many Southerners chose to move west to Texas, where they could also take their slaves, Northerners looked to the Oregon Country as their western destination. Well before the great movement along the Oregon Trail that involved thousands of covered wagons and tens of thousands of American migrants, a series of events drew the attention of many Americans to the region of the Willamette Valley in the Oregon Country. As early as 1792 an American ship captain named Robert Gray had visited the Oregon coast and sailed into the Columbia River, seeking trade with local Indians. He named the river after his ship, the *Columbia Rediva.* Gray carried with him a letter from President Washington, which was to serve as an introduction to any emperors or kings of the lands Gray might reach. Sailing up the Columbia, Gray soon traded several bolts of cloth and some sheets of copper with the local American Indians for 3,000 sea otter pelts. He also traded two nails for 600 beaver skins.

IMMIGRANTS TO AMERICA

During the 40-year span between 1790 and 1830, the population of the United States more than tripled, rising from 4 million to 13 million people. Nearly all of that growth was through natural increase—Americans having babies and large families. Only about 400,000 foreigners arrived in America during those decades. It would be in the years following 1830 that large numbers of immigrants began reaching American shores.

In the decade of the 1840s, over 1.5 million immigrants came to settle in the United States. Nearly half of these people came from famine-stricken Ireland. In the 1850s, well over 2.3 million more people saw the hope of new opportunity in the land west of the Atlantic. Why did so many people come to America during these years? There are many answers. As mentioned, a great famine struck Ireland in 1846. This, added to the poor working conditions, brought tens of thousands of people to the States. From Germany, thousands fled their homeland during the years 1848–49, when a revolution against political oppression failed.

Many other Europeans came to America to make their fortunes, or

Other Americans followed. In 1811 John Jacob Astor from New York established a trading post at the mouth of the Columbia River, called Fort Astoria. Across the river was a British fur post, called Fort Vancouver. By the 1820s and 1830s, a number of fur trappers had moved up the Missouri River from St. Louis, following the path of the Lewis and Clark Expedition, and into the wooded mountain regions in search of beaver furs.

Meanwhile, back East, campaigns launched by missionary societies and emigrant organizations were encouraging people to move to Oregon. In 1831, Hall Jackson Kelley established one such emigration society to promote permanent settlement in Oregon. He advertised in several eastern

at least to improve their economic futures. Most new immigrants became U.S. citizens shortly after arriving. They made their contributions to the new land mainly by farming and by establishing businesses. These new citizens could be found not only in big cities, such as New York, Philadelphia, and Boston, but also in the West, where they migrated for land and gold. The chart below shows the immigration pattern established during the decades from 1820 to 1860 by those who came to America from the British Isles, Ireland, Germany, and Scandinavia. These nations were among those whose people flocked to the United States.

Major European Immigration to the United States, 1821–60				
	1821–30	**1831–40**	**1841–50**	**1851–60**
Ireland	50,000	207,000	780,000	914,000
Britain (England, Scotland, Wales)	25,000	75,800	267,000	424,000
Germany	6,800	152,000	435,000	951,000
Scandinavia	260	2,260	14,440	24,680

New Arrivals in Oregon, 1840s

The Whitmans welcomed the arrival of new emigrants to their mission, which was set up near present-day Walla Walla, Washington. Most came by ox- and horse-drawn wagons. The 2,000-mile (3,200-kilometer) journey took up to six months. The emigrants brought with them only what they needed for the trip and to set up their new homes. The Indians soon became overwhelmed by the arrivals. Some even died of diseases carried by the emigrants. Inevitably, this led to conflict and confrontation.

publications and spoke to interested crowds, lecturing on the benefits of moving west. Another organizer was Nathaniel Wyeth, who extolled the rewards of traveling west along an overland route.

Wagons Ho!

One of the first missionary efforts began in Oregon when Jason Lee, a Methodist missionary traveling to Oregon with Nathaniel Wyeth, established an American settlement in 1834. Dr. Marcus Whitman and his young wife, Narcissa, were perhaps the most famous missionary couple to move to Oregon, taking up residence in the Walla Walla region in 1836. The Whitmans were led along the trail by fur trappers and traders and Narcissa was one of the first white women to travel the length of the western route, soon to be called the Oregon Trail. Although their missionary efforts generally failed, the Whitman mission became a notable stop for emigrants on the far western end of the Oregon Trail, until the couple were killed in 1847 by local Cayuse Indians.

In 1841 the first true wagon train, consisting of a dozen wagons and 70 settlers, traveled along the Oregon Trail to establish farms and settlements beside Oregon's Willamette River. Before the decade was over, more than 100,000 pioneers had settled in Oregon.

As early as 1843, Americans in Oregon were organizing a provisional government, with the intent to petition Congress for possible annexation and eventual statehood. The following year the Democrat candidate for president, James Knox Polk, a Jackson-like politician from Tennessee, ran on dual promises to annex Texas and the Oregon Country. In fact, Polk wanted an American Oregon that extended to the line of north latitude 54 degrees, 40 minutes, which was close to the actual border of Russian Alaska. His slogan, "Fifty-four Forty or Fight!" made his jingoistic intentions ring loud and clear. Once he became president, however, Polk reduced his reach and, after negotiating with the British, accepted the 49th parallel for Oregon, the one that separates Canada and the western United States today.

THE MEXICAN-AMERICAN WAR

Although Texas had gained its independence from Mexico in 1836, the Republic of Texas remained a separate nation until 1845, when it was annexed into the Union as an American state. Following that annexation, the unfriendly relations between Mexico and the United States worsened. The Mexican government bristled at the American move, and war between the two nations seemed inevitable. Officially, the cause of the Mexican–American War was a boundary dispute between the two countries. While the United States claimed the southern boundary of Texas to be the Rio Grande, Mexico insisted that the more northern Nueces River was the true dividing line.

In January 1846, President Polk sent U.S. General Zachary Taylor and 3,500 men to Texas to establish an encampment along the northern bank of the Rio Grande, a move that placed them, in the view of the Mexican government, on Mexican soil. Polk hoped he could goad the Mexicans into a war. On April 24, 1846, the Mexicans obliged, crossing the Rio Grande and killing or wounding 16 U.S. soldiers. Polk went immediately to Congress and requested a declaration of war, which he got on May 13. The Mexican–American War had commenced.

Zachary Taylor was the commanding U.S. officer in the war effort. He was in his 60s, having fought in the War of 1812, the Black Hawk War, and the Seminole Wars with Jackson. Known as "Old Rough and Ready," Taylor was well liked by his soldiers for his courage and easy-going manner. His strategy was to take the Mexican town of Monterrey and then march south to Mexico City. After a hard fight, Monterrey fell to Taylor. Then President Polk, feeling Taylor lacked the ability to lead an offensive against Mexico City, replaced him with General Winfield Scott. Upon taking command, Scott began marching his army down the eastern coast of Mexico. His troops took the city of Tampico and then Vera Cruz, which was the most important Mexican port along the Gulf Coast. Meanwhile, to the north, U.S. military forces under the command of Colonel Stephen Austin had succeeded in capturing Santa Fe (in modern-day New Mexico). American troops had also captured major coastal cities in California.

From Vera Cruz, Scott began his campaign inland toward the Mexican capital. The Americans were met by a spirited resistance from Mexican armies. Once the American army arrived in the vicinity of Mexico City, Scott defeated the enemy at Chapultepec on September 13, 1847. Victory over the Mexican forces was complete. In the resulting Treaty of Guadalupe Hidalgo, which ended the war, Mexico lost its northern territories, stretching from California to Texas—a total of 529,000 square miles (1,370,000 square kilometers) of land. These lands would one day become the states of New Mexico, California, Arizona, Utah, and Nevada.

THE CALIFORNIA GOLD RUSH

Seemingly, no sooner had the Mexican government ceded the vast region of the Southwest—called the Mexican Cession—to the United States, then the region of northern California yielded surprising discoveries. A Swiss immigrant called John Sutter had established a large ranch in the Sonoma Valley. In January 1848, one of his employees, James Marshall, was working on a new water mill when he saw the sparkle of glinting metal in the water of the mill's tailrace. He took the small bits to Sutter, who determined that they were indeed

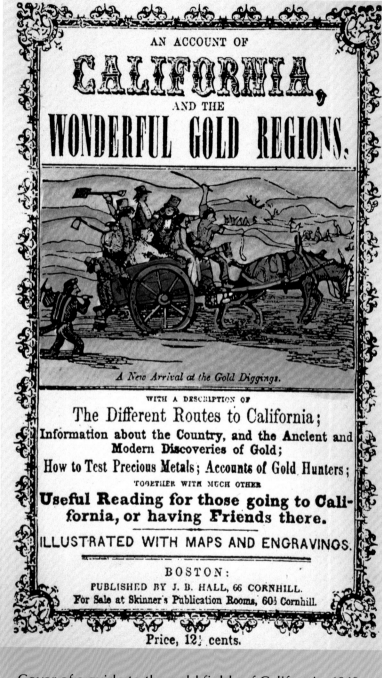

Cover of a guide to the gold fields of California, 1849.

gold. The two men agreed to keep the discovery a secret. But the news leaked out, and soon Americans were flocking west to California to seek their fortunes.

To some Americans, the discovery of gold on lands that had only recently been held by the Spanish seemed a gift from God himself. As noted by historian Lynn Perrigo, one American promoter wrote:

> *Why, Sir, did God preserve this whole country more than a century after its discovery for the English, turning the foot of the Spaniard to the sunny region of the tropics?... In fine, why were the immense treasures of California hidden from the world until she was annexed to this Republic? And tell me, if anyone can, why it was that the title deed of transference had no sooner passed into our hands than she gave up her mighty secret and unlocked her golden gates?*

Regardless, the great California Gold Rush was on. The Oregon Trail had seen a constant stream of emigrants through the 1840s, but now the tide became a torrent. The trail was crowded with several thousands of would-be miners, intent on getting out to California to make their fortune. With California as their destination, these emigrants followed the Oregon Trail to the area of the Great Salt Lake and then veered south on another route, known as the California Trail. Many others traveled by sea around South America. Such a trip was relatively safe and took about six months to complete, about as long as a trek on the trail across the West to California. Braver souls sailed south to the Isthmus of Panama, where they crossed the narrow strait to the western side and took passage on a ship heading north bound for San Francisco.

Once in the gold camps along the Sacramento and American Rivers, the lives of the prospectors proved difficult.

These men (along with a scattering of women) worked in local streams where they scooped up gravel in wide-brimmed pans, then swirled the water and lighter material out using centripetal force, hoping to leave the heavy metal behind as their golden yield. Gold fever and the increasing discovery of the metal brought inflation and higher costs for all of life's necessities. Miners needed to find close to one ounce (28 grams) of gold—then worth about $16—per day just to provide the basics for survival. Many went bust, finding little gold, but some did make their fortunes. The most permanent and far-reaching impact of the 1849 Gold Rush was that California became a state in 1850.

FROM THE ATLANTIC TO THE PACIFIC

When George Washington took the reins of the presidency in 1789 the United States was little more than a youthful republic, populated largely by farmers, who could not imagine their country extending from the Atlantic to the Pacific. However, within the three generations to follow, America had become a nation stretching across the continent, a country reliant on steam power and machines, where democracy itself had been redefined, and cities had sprung up across the landscape, planted in the wake of tens of thousands of Americans moving ever West.

Between 1789 and 1850 the United States had experienced two large-scale wars and a scattering of Indian conflicts, it had witnessed the births and deaths of several political parties, but it had emerged stronger and more nationalistic than ever. Reformers had retooled the nation's spiritual energies, while those who followed the lure of rich land in Oregon or golden riches in California had carried the American flag all the way to the western ocean. The reach of the United States had finally caught up with the distant footsteps of its earlier explorers, Lewis and Clark.

Yet the America created during the first 50 years of the nineteenth century had only deferred some of its flaws and failures. The institution of slavery grew through those decades until more than 4 million black men, women, and children were being held in perpetual bondage. It would remain for a future generation, one that would engage in the bloodiest war in U.S. history, to finally correct that fault.

Chronology

1789 Washington is inaugurated president and establishes his cabinet with Departments of State, War, and Treasury. The Judiciary Act of 1789 creates the Supreme Court with six justices and provides for lower courts. Tariff of 1789 (a protective tariff) is instituted. Congress submits the Bill of Rights for Ratification

TIMELINE

1789
Washington is inaugurated first president

1800
Thomas Jefferson becomes president

1809
James Madison becomes president

1812
President Madison asks Congress for a declaration of war against Great Britain

| 1789 | 1800 | 1810 | 1820 |

1794
The Whiskey Rebellion erupts in rural Pennsylvania

1803
Louisiana Purchase

1814
Washington City is burned by the British

1804
The Lewis and Clark Expedition begins

1817
James Monroe becomes president. Reelected in 1820

1790 Hamilton submits his Reports on Public Credit and outlines his financial program concerning the assumption of state debts

1791 The Bank of the United States is created. Hamilton submits his Report on Manufactures to Congress in which he calls for high tariff rates. Congress passes Whiskey Tax. Bill of Rights is ratified by the states

1792 American sea captain Robert Gray reaches the mouth of the Columbia River in Oregon

1793 Washington issues his Proclamation of Neutrality

1794 The Whiskey Rebellion erupts in rural Pennsylvania over whiskey tax. Washington calls out 13,000 troops

1824 John Quincy Adams becomes president

1828 Andrew Jackson elected president

1836 Martin Van Buren elected president

1850 California becomes an American state

1830 Indian Removal Act signed by President Jackson

1846 War opens between the United States and Mexico and ends in 1847

1821   **1830**   **1840**   **1850**

1825 Erie Canal is completed

1834 Nathaniel Wyeth establishes American settlement in Oregon

1841 First true wagon train reaches Oregon by way of the Oregon Trail

1848 Gold discovered in California

1795 Jay's Treaty with Britain is ratified by the Senate

1796 Pinckney's Treaty with Spain. Federalist John Adams is elected the nation's second president with Republican Thomas Jefferson as vice president

1797 XYZ Affair results in an undeclared naval war (Quasi War) with France

1798 The Alien and Sedition Acts are passed by Federalist Congress. Kentucky and Virginia Resolutions written by Thomas Jefferson and James Madison

1800 House of Representatives chooses Thomas Jefferson as president and Aaron Burr becomes vice president. The nation's capital is moved to Washington D.C., known then as Federal City

1801 John Marshall, a Federalist, is nominated Chief Justice of the Supreme Court by President Adams. "Midnight Appointees" chosen by President Adams lead to 1803 case Marbury v. Madison

1803 President Jefferson's diplomats make the Louisiana Purchase for $15 million

1804 The Lewis and Clark Expedition begins. George Rapp establishes the Rappites

1805 Napoleonic wars continue to disrupt American commercial shipping

1806 First Non-Importation act is passed by Congress. Lewis and Clark return from their trip across the West

1807 Leopard–Chesapeake Affair. Robert Fulton's steamboat, the *Clermont,* travels from New York City to Albany. Embargo Act requested by President Jefferson

1809 Non-Intercourse Act signed by President Jefferson. James Madison inaugurated as president. George Clinton is Vice President. Proclamation reinstating trade with Great Britain is issued by President

Madison. Madison reinstates Non-Intercourse Act

1811 New York entrepreneur John Jacob Astor establishes a fur trading post in Oregon

1812 President Madison asks Congress for a declaration of war against Great Britain. United States loses battle of Queenstown

1813 American forces burn the Canadian town of York. Oliver Hazard Perry defeats the British at the battle of Put-in-Bay, followed by American victory in battle of the Thames

1814 Washington City is burned by the British. The British fail to capture Fort McHenry. Hartford Convention secretly convenes. Treaty of Ghent signed by American and British peace commissioners

1815 Battle of New Orleans

1816 Second Bank of the United States established. "Era of Good Feelings" ushers in one-party system with the election of James Monroe as president

1817 Erie Canal project is begun

1819 Adams-Onis Treaty is signed, with Spain ceding East Florida to the United States while surrendering claims to West Florida

1820 President Monroe and Vice President Daniel Tompkins are elected to second term. Missouri Compromise hammered out by Henry Clay

1823 Monroe Doctrine presented to Congress

1824 Controversial election results in John Quincy Adams being made president

1825 Erie Canal is completed

1828 "The Tariff of Abominations" passes through Congress and is signed by President Adams. Andrew Jackson is elected president

1830 Indian Removal Act signed by President Jackson. Lowell Mills open

1831 Cherokee Nation v. Georgia. Cyrus McCormick invents automatic reaping machine. Hall Jackson Kelley establishes Oregon emigration society

1832 Worcester v. Georgia. Bill to recharter the Bank of the United States vetoed by President Jackson. South Carolina Ordinance of Nullification

1833 Jackson asks Congress to adopt a Force Bill to enable him to enforce the provisions of the Tariffs of 1828 and 1832. Compromise Tariff of 1833 drawn up by Henry Clay. Andrew Jackson is inaugurated for his second term

1833–37 Wild speculation in land, canals, and roads begins, carried out by "Wildcat Banks"

1834 Nathaniel Wyeth establishes American settlement in Oregon.

1836 Specie Circular issued by President Jackson. Martin Van Buren is elected president. Dr. Marcus and Narcissa Whitman establish a mission in Oregon Country. Samuel Colt invents the repeating revolver. Texans declare their independence from Mexico. Battle at the Alamo

1837 The Panic of 1837. John Deere develops the steel plow

1841 First true wagon train reaches Oregon by way of the Oregon Trail

1844 Samuel F. B. Morse invents the telegraph. James Knox Polk elected president

1846 War opens between the United States and Mexico. Elias Howe invents the sewing machine.

1847 Mexican–American War ends

1848 Women's rights convention held in Seneca Falls, New York. Gold discovered in California

1850 California becomes an American state

Glossary

aide-de-camp A military officer who serves a superior officer directly, often in his headquarters.

amendment An official change to an existing law or an existing document.

annexation Taking over complete control of the territory of another state or nation.

assimilation Renouncing or giving up one's previous cultural practices and replacing them with the practices of another culture.

assumption In finance, the taking over of an existing debt by a second party.

bunting A light cotton or woolen cloth, used to make flags.

caucus A closed meeting of the members of a political party or other organization at which important decisions are made.

celibate Refraining from sexual activity with another person.

confluence The meeting point of two or more rivers or streams.

coup The overthrow, usually by violent means, of an existing government by a group of citizens.

customs duties Money paid by an importer for the privilege of delivering one's goods for sale into a foreign country.

democracy Government by the people, exercised either directly or through elected representatives.

Democrats, Democratic Party One of the two major political parties in the United States, originating from a split in the Democratic-Republican Party under Andrew Jackson in 1828.

embargo A ban on trading goods with another country.

excise An internal or domestic tax.

executive privilege The power of an executive official, such as the president of the United States, to withhold information believed vital or crucial only to that official.

Founding Fathers The men who directed the establishment of the early United States as a country independent from Great Britain, including such important figures as George Washington, John Adams, and Thomas Jefferson.

francophile Someone who loves or admires all things French.

hulling Breaching the hull of a ship, as with cannon or artillery fire.

impressment The practice of kidnapping people and forcing them into service against their will.

judicial review The right of a court to determine the legitimacy or constitutionality of a law or other piece of legislation approved by a legislative body.

militia Soldiers recruited at a state level to serve the citizens of that state.

mutiny Open rebellion against an established authority, for example by soldiers or sailors against their superior officers.

nullification Declaring or considering something as non-binding.

pirogue French term for a type of flat-bottomed river craft, which featured a rudder and a mast.

polygamy The practice of a having more than one wife at a time.

precedent The establishment of a practice or tradition.

privateer A ship that is privately owned and manned, but authorized by a government during wartime to attack and capture enemy vessels.

republic Government in which supreme power resides in a body of citizens entitled to vote, and is exercised by elected officers and representatives responsible to them and governing according to law.

secession Making a complete political break from a former affiliation, by separating a state or province from a nation, for example.

specie Gold and silver used as money.

speculation The practice of buying or investing in a commodity, such as land, at a low price with the expectation of selling that commodity at a high level of profit.

temperance Abstinence from drinking alcoholic beverages.

theology The study of spiritual matters or religious practices and principles.

topography The varied lay of the land, including such features as mountains and valleys.

Trans-Appalachian West The region of North America that lies west of the Appalachian Mountains and extends to the Mississippi River.

Virginia Dynasty The run of early U.S. presidents who came from the state of Virginia, including Washington, Jefferson, Madison, and Monroe.

Bibliography

Barkun, Michael, *Crucible of the Millennium: Burned Over District of New York of the 1840s*. Syracuse, NY: Syracuse University Press, 1986.

Bassett, John Spencer, ed. *Correspondence of Andrew Jackson*. Washington, D.C.: Carnegie Institution of Washington, 1926–35.

Davis, David Brion. *The Boisterous Sea of Liberty: A Documentary History of America from Discovery Through the Civil War*. New York: Oxford University Press, 2000.

De Tocqueville, Alexis. *Democracy in America*. New York: Penguin Putnam, Inc., 2003

Fleming, Thomas. *The Louisiana Purchase*. Hoboken, NJ: John Wiley & Sons, 2003.

Flexner, James Thomas. *Washington: The Indispensable Man*. Boston: Little, Brown and Company, 1974.

Holloway, Mark. *Heavens on Earth: Utopian Communities in America, 1680–1880*. London: Turnstile Press, 1951.

Kluger, Richard. *Seizing Destiny: How America Grew from Sea to Shining Sea*. New York: Alfred A. Knopf, 2007.

Koch, Adrienne, and William Peden, ed. *The Life and Selected Writings of Thomas Jefferson*. New York: Random House. The Modern Library edition, 1972.

Langguth, A. J. *Union 1812: The Americans Who Fought the Second War of Independence*. New York: Simon & Schuster, 2007.

Moulton, Gary. *The Lewis and Clark Journals: An American Epic of Discovery*. An Abridgement of the Definitive Nebraska Edition. Lincoln: University of Nebraska Press, 2003.

Perrigo, Lynn. *The American Southwest: Its People and Cultures*. New York: Holt, Rinehart, and Winston, 1971.

Remini, Robert V. *A Short History of the United States*. New York: HarperCollins Publishers, 2008.

Reynolds, David S. *Waking Giant: America in the Age of Jackson*. New York: HarperCollins Publishers, 2008.

Schmidt, Thomas and Jeremy. *The Saga of Lewis & Clark: Into the Uncharted West*. New York: DK Publishing, Inc., 1999.

Siegerman, Harriet. *An Unfinished Battle: American Women, 1848–1865*. New York: Oxford University Press, 1998.

Thornton, Willis. *"The Day They Burned the Capitol."* American Heritage Magazine, December, 1954.

Toll, Ian W. *Six Frigates: The Epic History of the Founding of the U.S. Navy*. New York: W. W. Norton & Company, 2006.

Varon, Elizabeth. *Disunion!: The Coming of the American Civil War, 1789–1959*. Chapel Hill: University of North Carolina Press, 2008.

Weinstein, Allen. *The Story of America: Freedom and Crisis from Settlement to Superpower*. New York: DK Publishing Company, 2002.

Wilentz, Sean. *The Rise of American Democracy: Jefferson to Lincoln*. New York: W. W. Norton & Company, 2005.

Further Resources

Behrman, Carol. *John Adams*. Minneapolis: Lerner Publishing Group, 2004.

Capek, Michael. *Personal Tour of a Shaker Village*. Minneapolis: Lerner Publishing Group, 2001.

Doherty, Kieran. *Andrew Jackson*. New York: Scholastic Library Publishing, 2003.

Edelman, Rob. *The War of 1812*. San Diego: Gale Group, 2005.

Favor, Lesli J. *Martin Van Buren*. New York: Scholastic Library Publishing, 2003.

Feinbert, Barbara. *John Adams*. New York: Scholastic Library Publishing, 2003.

Hort, Lennie. *George Washington*. New York: DK Publishing, Inc., 2004.

January, Brendan. *George Washington*. New York: Scholastic Library Publishing, 2003.

January, Brendan. *James Madison*. New York: Scholastic Library Publishing, 2003.

Kudlinski, Kathleen V. *Facing West: A Story of the Oregon Trail*. New York: Penguin Young Readers Group, 1996.

Levine, Ellen. *If You Traveled West in a Covered Wagon*. New York: Scholastic, Inc., 1992.

McCollum, Sean. *John Quincy Adams*. New York: Scholastic Library Publishing, 2003.

McNeese, Tim. *Alamo*. Philadelphia: Chelsea House Publishers, 2003.

McNeese, Tim. *Alexander Hamilton: Framer of the Constitution*. New York: Chelsea House Publishers, 2006.

McNeese, Tim. *George Washington: America's Leader in War and Peace*. New York: Chelsea House Publishers, 2006.

Otfinoski, Steven. *William Henry Harrison*. New York: Scholastic Library Publishing, 2003.

Roop, Peter, and Connie Roop. *The Louisiana Purchase*. New York: Simon & Schuster Children's Publishing, 2004.

Santella, Andrew. *James Monroe*. New York: Scholastic Library Publishing, 2003.

Streissguth, Thomas. *Utopian Visionaries*. Minneapolis: Oliver Press, Inc., 1998.

Web sites

Amana Colonies:
http://www.amanacolonies.com/

American Presidents:
http://www.americanpresidents.org/

Historic New Harmony:
http://www.ulib.iupui.edu/kade/newharmony/home.html

Lewis and Clark:
http://www.lewis-clark.org/
http://www.nationalgeographic.com/west/

Louisiane Purchase:
http://www.louisianapurchase2003.com/

Mexican War and the Alamo:
http://www.lone-star.net/mall/texasinfo/mexicow.htm
http://www.thealamo.org/revolution.html

Monticello and Mount Vernon:
http://www.monticello.org/
http://www.mountvernon.org

Oregon Trail:
http://www.isu.edu/~trinmich/Oregontrail.html

Smithsonian—Star-Spangled Banner:
http://americanhistory.si.edu/starspangledbanner/

Transcendentalists:
http://www.transcendentalists.com/

U.S.–Mexican War:
http://www.pbs.org/kera/usmexicanwar/index_flash.html

Picture Credits

Index

About the Author

Tim McNeese is associate professor of history at York College in York, Nebraska. Professor McNeese holds degrees from York College, Harding University, and Missouri State University. He has published more than 100 books and educational materials. His writing has earned him a citation in the library reference work, *Contemporary Authors* and multiple citations in *Best Books for Young Teen Readers*. In 2006, Tim appeared on the History Channel program, *Risk Takers, History Makers: John Wesley Powell and the Grand Canyon*. He was been a faculty member at the Tony Hillerman Writers Conference in Albuquerque. His wife, Beverly, is assistant professor of English at York College. They have two married children, Noah and Summer, and three grandchildren—Ethan, Adrianna, and Finn William. Tim and Bev have sponsored college study trips on the Lewis and Clark Trail and to the American Southwest. You may contact Professor McNeese at tdmcneese@york.edu.

About the Consultant

Richard Jensen is Research Professor at Montana State University, Billings. He has published 11 books on a wide range of topics in American political, social, military, and economic history, as well as computer methods. After taking a Ph.D. at Yale in 1966, he taught at numerous universities, including Washington, Michigan, Harvard, Illinois-Chicago, West Point, and Moscow State University in Russia.